# IF THIS IS THE CAVALRY, WHERE ARE ALL THE HORSES?

## Leroy E. Durkin

PublishAmerica
Baltimore

First printing

ISBN: 1-4137-5374-4
PUBLISHED BY PUBLISHAMERICA, LLLP
www.publishamerica.com
Baltimore

Printed in the United States of America

# DEDICATION

*"The highest honor I have ever attained is that of having my name Coupled with yours."*

-General George Patton

This book is for my inimitable wife, Mildred—she taught me well. The people in this book may have formed my life, but my wonderful wife gave it substance.

The ghosts of our past parades—those whose lives have left only the words—to all of you this book is dedicated.

Last but never least—Jimmy Durkin, Blanche Beatrice Durkin, Edna Durkin, my daughter Linda Lou and grandchildren—Durkins past, present and future...remember always, you are loved.

-Dear old Dad aka Pop

# FOREWORD

To look back on a special time in someone's life is a gift. With this book my father has allowed us to not only share in his journey as a young man through war, but has graced us with the memories and men who were his lifeline during World War II.

A story of humor and sorrow. Lessons learned at such an early age which carried him forward to live a spectacular life of kindness and trust.

For all who have known Leroy—we say thank you, Dad, for everything.... For those of you he has not met, suffice to say, the world is a better place for his presence in ours.

-Linda Durkin Richardson

# CONTENTS

# PROLOGUE

From a very early age my grandchildren have been unusually inquisitive. "What did you do in the big war, Poppie?" was always good for an old tale retold, or an occasional new one recounted after a Company D reunion.

Durk and Tim, my youngest grandsons, are a great audience. Once in a while they question the veracity or time frame of a story but they always seem to enjoy the camaraderie. Granddaughter Samantha (who was college-bound when I began this work and has now graduated) believed my memoirs should be written to share with grandsons Pat and Hoa, now middle-aged family men (just joking, guys). They had fled the nest for college by the time I retired, which is when I began telling war stories at great length. I also wanted to share once again the experiences of a lifetime with those old buddies still surviving.

Sami's final bit of advice was, "Delete the embellishments, Pop!" And so it begins.

# 1

# FORT DIX

It was an extremely cold February morning in 1943 when our locomotive finally pulled out of the Millville, New Jersey, station. Most of us had been on the platform since 5 a.m., waiting for the stationmaster to back the train into the station to begin the trip to Fort Dix and our future.

When we were finally permitted to board the train it was obvious to everyone that the doors had been left open during the night. They remained open as we pulled out of the yard, creating an arctic wind blowing through the cars. The coaches appeared to be relics from the Civil War.

Leaving behind a station full of emotional relatives, we noticed it had begun snowing. The group in my car was subdued, each man engrossed in his own thoughts. My mind went back to conversations with my dad about his experiences in World War I. I liked it best when Dad told me how he moved up through the ranks from private to buck sergeant. He never allowed a soldier under his command to be surly, slow acting or a wise guy, he said. They learned what "that's an order" meant very quickly.

"Son, if—God forbid—you are ever in the service, work hard!" he had said. "Don't horse around; go for as many stripes as you can, and remind yourself—RHIP." "Rank has its privileges" was an idea he had drummed into me, especially after Pearl Harbor.

Like every other red-blooded American, I had immediately wanted to join up. My first wartime task, however, had been getting reclassified. I was an assistant foreman at Dupont, an essential war industry, manufacturing artificial neoprene rubber. It had taken months of persistent requests and veiled threats before I finally had been released. Just three days later, I was en route to Fort Dix for my physical and mental evaluations.

We seemed to stop at every town and cattle crossing but eventually we reached our destination. At the depot we were loaded into eight open army trucks exposed to the elements—in other words, into a bone-chilling snowstorm.

Upon our arrival at the barracks we were off-loaded from the trucks, then ordered to turn and face the sergeant. His name, he said, was Staff Sergeant Leibeck and he had just been written-up in *Life Magazine* as the toughest drill sergeant in the U.S. Army. He personally "vas going to march us into der chow hall" —a new name for a place to eat—then he'd take us to our "lovely bungalow, var ve vood all take a shower and take the first empty sack"—a new word for a bed. "Und ve vill not be awakened until 5 a.m. at vitch time ve vood hear his melodious voice und his vissel" (whistle) requesting that we all fall into the exact spot that we now occupied.

Staff Sergeant Leibeck, ve soon learned, vas Polish, und his English, ve all agreed, vas shitty, to use one of his own favorite words. "If ve ver late, he vould chew each vone of us a brant-new bung hole."

Our first army meal consisted of black-eyed peas, bacon, beans, and a stale roll with a slightly red hamburger. Dessert was an ugly, watery, red-colored Jell-o.

I remember getting into my sack that night and looking back on my first army day—the cold weather, the train ride, the lousy meal, being insulted by a big nasty Pole and winding up in a very cold barracks with twenty-six toilets and long rows of double-decker bunks. At which point some total jackass tried to blow taps on a dented, out-of-tune bugle. Said bugle told me to close my eyes and go to sleep. But as soon as the lights went out a few crybaby recruits began to sniffle and whine about how they wished they were in their own beds, not these damned upper cots that you are afraid to sleep in and fall the hell out of, or worse still, you have the bottom bunk and someone wets the bed and possibly soaks unlucky you!

True to Sergeant Leibeck's word, at 4:30 we were awakened by his raucous voice and whistle, which seemed to have the same resonance. Each time he blew that damned thing, it was like a rusty bayonet being held to our throats. The snow and sleet had stopped, but the wind was a cutting blast, and the bitter cold and the continual blackout conditions made things very gloomy. Add to this we were under the control—not supervision but *control*—of a wild SOB whom our company soon gave the nickname "Sergeant Psycho." Sergeant Psycho seemed to tower over all of us rookies. He was a tall, lanky tough-looking man, gruff and scary as hell to the whole company.

That first morning in particular, the sergeant seemed to lose it. The psycho screamed at us to line up, in a straight line, at attention, with no noise. "I vant quiet, damn you no-brains und stupid shit heads." There we were, standing in the cold at rigid and very tense attention, when one of the men fainted, fell forward into the next line, and knocked two other recruits out of line, screwing up the formation. After removal of the fainted recruit Staff Sergeant Leibeck spent the next fifteen minutes chewing us all out. "The next time one of you numb-nuts thinks that you are going to faint, you will get the hell out of my formation, even if you have to crawl out through six feet of snow."

He seemed to stare at each one of us individually as he yelled, "You screw up my formation, you will spend a full week peeling potatoes, scrubbing pots and pans, and cleaning the kitchen grease pit" (the dirtiest job in the camp). *"Listen up.* You men are no longer rookies. You think you are being manipulated unnecessarily; plus you have lost your status as American civilians. You are wrong. You have been given the honor of protecting your country, your families, your religion. You think your sergeants and officers or my orders are idiotic, you think they are maniacs in the field? Them being maniacs will probably save your life in the future!"

We still hadn't broken ranks for breakfast. Sergeant Leibeck finally said, "If you think you need to complain about something, you ask for permission to see me, or you ask for Staff Sergeant Bronski. And you better not give us any BS or ask for any favors. You are numb-nuts, today, tomorrow and as long as you are under my command. Now listen up. You will be called to attention. Then fall out, then a standard set of orders after fallout. You have twenty minutes for breakfast and sick call, and you numb-nuts better not fake it. We've had more than a few guys that thought they were sick until Sergeant Bronski explained what the hell the army considers sick."

Sergeant Bronski was happy to tell us: "Ya gotta be bleedin' a lot or have pneumonia in an advanced stage. If ya ain't in any of these conditions, then ya ain't frigging sick!" We soon learned that the rest of the U.S. Army used exactly the same standards for sick call.

Sergeant Bronski advised us that we were to rush through our breakfast, as we would be getting shots for almost every known disease that could be caught in America, Europe, China, or the islands of the Pacific. No one knew or cared where we were going to be shipped, so the rule was "shoot 'em up" for each and every area of the world where anyone was firing a gun.

We were told we would fall out at 2 a.m. with all of our gear packed (truly, jammed) into our duffel bags, leaving our barracks and surrounding area spic-and-span clean. We actually heard the sergeant's whistle at 2:15 a.m., fell out for breakfast, cleaned up, and began marching to the rail yard to board another cold train at 10 a.m. Hooked onto one hell of a big locomotive, it finally pulled out of the yard at 5 p.m. on a very dismal evening—destination unknown. A young second lieutenant onboard, who had just graduated as a ninety-day wonder, informed me that this was a "secrecy movement act." We were on our way to war!

We spent eight full days on what seemed to be the dirtiest coal locomotive the U.S. Army could find. Each coach car had a one-closet toilet. Our new army uniforms became stiff from coal soot. Each coach had been assigned one MP whose job it was, nobody knew. However, when our troop train stopped at Washington, D.C.'s yard, we learned some more army abbreviations—AWOL and MP's.

We finally ended up in a very dirty freight yard in El Paso, Texas.

14

It obviously didn't need yet another large coal locomotive such as ours spouting pure soot. But that's where our second lieutenant was given charge of us for exercise. We were off-loaded at the back end of the yard to spend an hour and a half first running fifty yards, then walking 150 yards. Around and around the whole frigging filthy freight yard. With promises of future baths and clean uniforms, we were reloaded onto our train, which had been cleaned, and with a loud "toot, toot" we were on our way to Camp Stewart, Georgia. That took another four and a half days of dirty, smoky soot, along with piss-poor meals of cold cans of C rations. The only good times were at the water stops, when the Red Cross and Salvation Army delivered hot coffee, chocolate and doughnuts.

We were young, healthy, keyed up and ready for basic training. At least that's what we thought!

# 2

# FROM CAMP STEWART TO FORT DEVENS

It was 2 a.m. when the train pulled into Camp Stewart's terminal. We were off-loaded, lined up and trucked to our assigned barracks. There we were ordered to shower and to be ready to fall out in our fatigues in twenty minutes, ready for work details that would be assigned by our new noncoms. We soon discovered these were cadre from Tennessee, South Carolina, Georgia, Texas, Virginia—all good-old Southern boys, hard-as-nails, no-nonsense sergeants. They were there for one reason only—to make capable, alert soldiers out of us.

It turned out that our cadre were themselves mostly rookies who had arrived three days before us. They had spent the prior two months on very tough maneuvers in the mountains of West Virginia. Having had our asses kicked by Sergeants Leibeck and Bronski, we were not much in awe of them. But they included big, strong, alert corporals, sergeants and one very knowledgeable first sergeant, who had earned his stripes prior to Pearl Harbor. This one had heard every sad story ever told by a recruit, and knew all of the weird answers, including a few he had made up himself

After a couple of weeks training we learned that our cadre would not be assigned as our permanent leaders, but would be reassigned to other outfits as permanent teaching cadres. That meant that, although most of our officers would stay with us, our noncoms would be promoted from our own ranks. I immediately thought of Dad and RHIP

I asked for permission to speak to our first sergeant and told him about the training I had received from Sergeant Jimmy Durkin of the First World War, with his 1903 rifle and his knowledge of flanking movements, the proper way to salute officers, etc. First Sergeant Damato asked a few questions. Having followed my dad's instructions I had learned my army serial number (I still know it: 32750111) and the serial number of my rifle. These I readily gave to the first sergeant, who then sent me to my barracks to return with my rifle, which he checked for oil and dust, then for the serial number he had written on his pad. Finding everything in order, he had me follow him out to the parade ground and rammed me through the total Manual of Arms a few times. I managed to perform without errors.

That's all it took to be given the immediate rank of temporary corporal. I was assigned to teach a squad of my buddies the rudiments of the Manual of Arms. One of the men kept referring to his rifle as his "gun," which is of course unacceptable. I had him repeat the long-famous army poem until the complete squad memorized it:

*"This is my rifle, this is my gun.*
*This one's for fighting, and this one's for fun."*

I sat the squad down and explained to them that our future was in our hands. Our best option was to learn together and instantly follow orders until our squad was the best in the company in the art of marching and drills. From then on, we used most of our spare time mastering the contents of the military manual. We continually did the Manual of Arms while marching. Within a week my squad was the pride of our company, praised by our colonel after we were given the honor of marching as a squad and performing a silent drill with rifles. My first sergeant was authorized to process the order making Corporal Durkin a buck sergeant. I asked that Private Joe Smith be made a gun-commander and be promoted to corporal of track one. Joe Smith was promoted the next day to corporal, and we spent three hours that night with our squad at the local PX, drinking 2.3 beer and celebrating.

\* \* \*

During the summer months, Camp Stewart, Georgia, was coated with a heavy, red dust. Most of our training took place in sections of a great swamp, which we shared with a few trillion mosquitoes. Each rainy morning I warned the troops at roll call that "Sure as hell we are going on a ten- or twelve-mile hike into the great swamp." And sure as hell, we'd go! And every morning I'd warn the troops that "No one under any circumstances is to drink any swamp water, regardless of how thirsty they are or how clear the pool or stream might appear." Despite that, three sad sacks from the first platoon ended up in the hospital, listed as near death's door. They had all taken drinks from what they thought was a sparkling pure pool of water. One sad sack who disobeyed my order not to drink retained the nickname of "Swampwater" for the balance of the war.

When Swampwater was released from the hospital, he was placed on limited duty. I recommended to my captain that we transfer or trade him ASAP because as a "GFU" (General F\*\*\*- up) he would reduce the efficiency of our unit. The captain was annoyed by the idea that there was such a thing as a soldier that he/we could not whip into shape, even though it was common knowledge that there existed, by definition, at least, one outstanding GFU in every unit of the Army, Navy, Marines, Air Corps and Coast Guard. He decided to pass the problem on to our new executive officer, seeing as how the primary reason for the executive officer's existence was to clean up, unload, or swap-transfer, as soon as possible, all possible misfits, malcontents, screw-ups, and pain-in-the-ass characters. Of course he didn't want the unlucky new XO to know to what extent he was being used.

\* \* \*

With my new buck sergeant rate, it was not rare for me to advise an occasional cadre noncom to back off from my platoon noncoms. Especially when one of the cadre defined a college boy as anyone older than eighteen who could read without moving his lips. This silly statement had been uttered behind the back of one of our very new second lieutenants. Naturally, he took umbrage at the remark and asked me to explain the facts of life to the cadre noncoms. We should all be aware, he said, that the cadre currently serving under him, although physically capable, were not of sufficient intelligence to lead our company into combat. One of his own trainees would eventually be tapped.

\* \* \*

We now belonged to the 491st Coast Artillery Battalion (antiaircraft automatic weapons—semi-mobile). Half-tracks (armored vehicles with truck tires in the front and tank-like treads in the back) had replaced the horses, but we were still the cavalry!

\* \* \*

It was one hell of a hot day in Georgia and Company D had just finished marching twelve miles out of camp on some very dusty, yellow, gravel-dirt roads. We rested for a half hour, during which we had some C rations and nasty-tasting, tepid canteen water. Then I blew the whistle and we began the twelve-mile return to camp on the same tree-less, shade-less roads.

During the half hour of rest, Lieutenant Viola, our platoon leader, had informed me that I had done a very good job counting cadence from the back of the troops. The rhythm of counting cadence helps troops maintain a more relaxed, no-strain march, as a full unit, a part of the whole, not as single soldiers and definitely not as civilians. As

19

we returned to camp, the men started copying my "hup-tup-trip-fo."
As I swung over to one of Dad' s marching songs, they all joined in
tune and cadence, "I got a girl in Salt Lake City—Sound off—Sound
off—Two cork legs and ain't she pretty—Sound off."

Cadence counting was occasionally interrupted by my cry from the
rear of the troops, "Close it up. Stop bouncing. Get off that rubber ball.
Keep your interval. Close it up. Hup-two. Close it up. Sound off,
cadence count, one, two, three, four—three, four." With my voice
made hoarse by the dusty choking yellow Georgia dust, we marched
up our company street. I started very loudly, "Sound off, cadence
count—one, two, three, four—three, four. To the left flank, ho. To the
right flank, ho—Forward march, Hup. To the left flank, ho—
Company—Halt—one, two—Dress right—Ten-hut."

The company had stopped in unison and correctly, at attention
before our captain. Lieutenant Viola indicated a job well done. Our
captain called out, "At ease. Sergeant Durkin—front and center."
The captain was facing the troops and he motioned for me to face him
with my back to the troops. I saluted him. He returned the salute and
he said, loud enough for all to hear, "Sergeant Durkin, that was a very
well-controlled march." He saluted me, which took me by surprise,
and said to me and the troops, "Ten-hut. *First* Sergeant Durkin will
dismiss you for chow." I took a fast glance at Lieutenant Viola, called
the company to attention, saluted our captain, did an about-face, and
as soon as the captain vacated the scene gave the company an "at
ease" order. I then thanked them for being a fine, capable body of
soldiers, and dismissed them for chow.

To be a first sergeant of very good men during wartime surpassed
anything I could imagine. I still feel that way. When I entered my tent
and stood in front of an old mirror, I asked myself—did I look old
enough, strong enough, or hard enough? I bared my teeth in a snarl,
made a deep growl, buckled on my .45 automatic, stood sideways to
the mirror, gun in hand, imagining how my arm, with its stripes of "three
up and three down," plus its diamond in the middle, would look—when
my .45 automatic accidentally went off, blowing the mirror into many
pieces.

Swiftly sticking my head out of the tent, I heaved a gigantic sigh of relief at not seeing anyone running in my direction. I assumed no one gave a damn if I had accidentally shot myself. Or better still, if someone had killed the SOB who was sure to be a pain in the ass, new First Sergeant Durkin.

Up until that day three of our companies had been using "acting first sergeants." One of the acting first sergeants had been returned to his place in the regular U.S. Infantry, which is why I got the sudden promotion.

Lieutenant Viola's congratulations included these words of wisdom: "From now on you will be under constant surveillance by your men and all officers. What you think will be known, what you speak will be heard, and what you do will be seen. Always keep that foremost in your mind!"

\* \* \*

While at Camp Stewart, Corporal Joe Smith proved himself a very capable and intelligent noncom. His men, guns and equipment were always clean and available for any officer's surprise inspection. We spent a lot of our time studying *The Soldier's Weapons Manuals* together until we were as knowledgeable as the people who wrote them. We also spent time training the squad members "mano y mano" (one on one) almost every day on the range. And we practiced firing a 40mm Bofars cannon at targets being towed behind twin-engine A-20s, medium bombers that flew from our left and usually at 2,000 feet, for about a quarter of a mile.

Their rate of air speed was 120 miles per hour, which didn't leave our gun crews too much time to sight and estimate the changing target height, distance, speed, etc. Orders were that the 40mm Bofar gun should be in a revetment, a barricade constructed to protect it from explosives. Six paces away from the gun was the section's power motor and fire control director, a metal-encased unit supported by a tripod and fitted with both a range finder and telescopic sights, with a man on each scope. These men tracked the target, one for distance

21

and the other for height. The director was synchronized with the gun so that its electronic data automatically controlled the gun's aiming and tracking patterns. When the corporal engaged the gun to the director, the cannon was capable of firing 120 rounds per minute. Each point was a detonating projectile, containing sixteen ounces of nitro cellulose. We were also capable of using the 40mm as an anti-tank gun with our armor-piercing rounds.

We also fired four .50 caliber synchronized machine guns. Our half-tracks held the self-contained electronic equipment that automatically zeroed in on the target, with possible bursts of 3,200 rounds per minute. On the range Corporal Joe proved that he and his crew had not been asleep during their classes. His crew scored the most points, by being on the target first and then being most alert to the range officers. Joe's reward was a promotion to chief of section, a buck sergeant.

* * *

To "move up the ladder," be made almost ready for combat, the First Battalion was to be shipped to Fort Devens, Mass. There we would fire our heavy guns at targets to be towed behind PT boats. But our trip was interrupted by what was supposed to be a six-week layover on Long Island, where we were positioned as antiaircraft protection around the P-47 Douglas aircraft plant and airfield. In our second week there, I was putting my two crews, one on each end of the runway, through sets of maneuvers involving a combat-simulated strafe from the north end of the field. I received a call alerting us that two flights of three P-47 fighter planes each would be practicing strafing. Also, to prove their bombing accuracy, they would try to splatter our crews and guns with small packages of flour they would drop. The first flight would be a sneak raid on the deck from the southern end of the field.

Our orders were to track each plane with our guns and to simulate shooting them down with both our 40mm Bofars and the quad's .50 caliber guns. Units had been equipped with cameras that would record both the fighters and the antiaircraft's ability to lead the fighters so that they would fly into our simulated firing patterns. I had assumed a position atop the gun's revetment with my field glasses focused on the southern end of the field, when I suddenly saw activity at the southern gun crew's area. I alerted my station and we moved away from the middle of the revetment, out of their field of fire. As the P-47s swept down towards us, seemingly about ten feet above the airfield, I sensed that I could look right over the middle fighter and that he was mere inches above the concrete runway. I realized that I needed to jump into the revetment with my gun crew or I would be decapitated in mere seconds. However, before I could move it became obvious that all three pilots had started their pull-up, a screaming, roaring climb in a very tight maneuver with all of our guns following their climb upward without any change of their controlled aim.

I began to climb back on the top of the revetment. I turned with my glasses and followed them upward until they began to slow in their climb—approaching their stalling speeds. My crew watched as their point man rolled over into "a split-ass maneuver" and began to fly at crazy, full-powered speed down toward our position in his simulated strafing and flour-bombing run.

In a few moments, and for no apparent reason, his wingmen did not complete their split-ass but instead rolled over and pulled out of their two positions, one going left, the other right. However, the leader was holding center very, very large and did not seem to be pulling back on his stick. He seemed intent on obliterating not just his life but also the lives of my men and me. At the last possible second I went head first into the revetment as I felt the hot wind being pushed ahead of the plane. It barely missed the ends of our gun barrel and revetment and crashed about thirty yards past us, disintegrating as it exploded, and kept moving down the runway. I immediately climbed from the revetment and with two other men chased the disintegrating plane, hopeful that the pilot would somehow escape and live. One of the engines, because of its weight, broke loose at this time. We were running as fast as possible, with the plane a hundred or so yards in front of us, when a parachute suddenly exploded out of the sliding wreckage.

We changed our running direction and followed the parachute, which proved to be still attached to the pilot's body. However, as the momentum of the wreckage began to slow down in its mad scattering of ever smaller pieces, we realized that the chute had not opened but had become a dragging, long, dirty white cloth burning in spots and pulling the dead pilot from his cockpit section of the destroyed plane. Except for the screeching from the engine still bouncing toward the middle of the tarmac, there was a deathly stillness as we approached the horribly mangled body of the very young pilot—our first casualty.

The other two planes pulled up and landed at another field. The next day my captain and I, along with the number eight gun crew, were summoned to battalion headquarters as on-the-spot witnesses to the crash. Two days later we were pulled out and loaded on trains for a fast trip to Fort Devens.

* * *

Our final training in the U.S. consisted of firing on towed marine targets using 40mm .50 caliber quads under strident combat conditions. Those conditions included the company being called up for a ball-breaking series of night exercises. We also had a final period of training with maps, compasses and map overlays. This period was then tied into one final over-the-bay antiaircraft firing. Twin-motor A-20 medium bombers towed targets for each 40mm. Our crews were to receive an alert call, then rush to their 40mm or to their half-tracks, utilizing speed and caution (four synchronized .50 caliber machine guns), sight their directors onto the plane's target, and connect the weapons and directors. Not hitting the airplane resulted in being called a frigging blind bunch of stupid bastards. I always maintained that our officers' screaming, pointing, and cussing made them seem like a couple of old madams who had been made aware of their total lack of taste at a hookers' international convention.

We were lucky to achieve an exceptional targets-hit score. Two days after that antiaircraft exercise, the Navy called to alert our battalion that we were to be lined up along the shoreline of the bay to fire on targets being towed behind PT boats about a half mile to our right, moving to our left at approximately twelve to fourteen miles per hour. No automatic fire from the 40mm Bofors would be authorized and every gun had to be zeroed in on the range finder electric director. Each gun was to expend five rounds and have each round zeroed in by their respective half-mile range. At the end of the five-round practice, all guns were to be cleared.

It was a beautiful sunny day. The bay was calm, our five-round exercise was perfect, and no incidents were noted during the clearing of the weapons. But the first PT boats began to cross in front of us at about eight miles per hour, five miles slower than the director and guns had been calibrated for. Our captain and his executive officer commanded and counter commanded, cussed and screamed. The sergeant in charge tried to change the calibration while in action, an absolute no-no. Two of the 40mms moved up the towing cable, cutting the cable, and then moved over the first PT's deck, erupting into a series of small splashes about 150 yards on the other side of the PT. This caused the captains of the PTs to open their throttles, spin their wheels and head for "blue waters and safety."

Although we passed with a score of eighty-five percent of our firing missions, we were really too dangerous with any gun to be given a good rating. I think gun crew number eight was actually called "certifiable cretin." However, we were approved for overseas combat. SHAEF (Supreme Headquarters Allied Expeditionary Force)—here we come!

# 3

# ON BOARD THE *QUEEN MARY*

Our battalion was hurriedly convoyed back to Fort Dix, quarantined, and given orders to be ready for shipment to England on the *Queen Mary's* next return trip. The excitement ran high among all the men, except for a very few who had been talking AWOL These shirkers were sent to the stockade for their own safety until the actual loading of the ship began. They would then be broken a rank, but they would still accompany their companies—without "any more crap!"

I was very proud to be the first sergeant of Company D and going overseas at last. We boarded the *Queen* with very little confusion, due to a company of engineers that was responsible for the stowing of our equipment, trucks, tracks, jeeps, guns, etc. As we went up the gangplank, a band was playing "The Jersey Bounce." We left port on Easter Sunday, 1943, escorted by two destroyers. They helped open the submarine-steel-net that stretched across the mouth of New York Harbor, and as we passed Ellis Island and the Statue of Liberty there was not a sound from the men crowding onto the deck.

It was as though we had all realized at the same time where we were going and why, that some of our futures were bleak, and that a mighty enemy was waiting for the chance to terminate the unlucky ones. We had no cockiness. We pretended nothing. We knew that we had no real future. We lived wholly and completely in the present. We expected prolonged exposure to future dangers and the repeated possible experience of seeing some of our friends torn brutally apart. We knew that we would seldom wash, rarely sleep, and never wake with any hope beyond the next few hours. We were irrevocably removed from inconsequentialities. Men who have been in combat, even those who escape unscathed, are somehow set apart ever afterwards from their own previous lives.

As a first sergeant I did not bunk with my men. I was assigned to a cabin with the other top-kicks. However, I spent most of the trip with my men, wondering if we would ever see the Statue of Liberty again. Some of the men were convinced that their potential for survival was negative.

On the third day out, we ran into a storm and many, many, men became extremely seasick. Some men who could take the rough seas still became sick because some dirty dog would smoke a cigar and blow the smoke into their faces. As luck would have it, this was also the day we were fed kidney pie and clam stew. Hell, even the guys who lived in Cape Cod and loved clam stew couldn't fake it! The *Queen Mary* was big, but as one of the *Queen's* officers told me, in comparison to a storm she was just a little cork.

\* \* \*

On our second day out, with the pre-storm winds getting fairly gusty, many of the passengers were shooting craps or playing cards. Others lined the ship's rails, wistfully looking back towards home, no doubt with bleak personal thoughts about their futures. It was cold and I was wearing a clean new field jacket with my first sergeant's stripes, plus a heavy brown sweater that my dad had sent to me. The wind blowing over the bow was cold as hell, and it started to rain.

I had been standing under the overhang, talking to a First Lieutenant Greenberg who had worked his way through Temple University and in his sophomore year joined the U.S. Army reserves. He had worked his way up to the rank of first sergeant in his senior year and got his second lieutenant's bar upon graduation. We agreed that the best rank in the army was first sergeant because RHIP.

Lieutenant Greenberg had a great story. Here is what he told me:

"I graduated from Temple University with honors, and was immediately posted as a second lieutenant in the real horse cavalry at the Delaware Water Gap. I had never seen a horse up close before and the way they looked at me and shrugged their long necks and shoulders wasn't encouraging. I knew I was never going to be able to climb up on these great big hairy beasts and control them.

"When I reported to battalion for assignment I was introduced to the first sergeant. He offered to teach me the rudiments. He introduced me to my assigned horse and showed me how to handle, curry, and comb him. He showed me how to clean a stall 'without getting your ass kicked by accident or on purpose.' After one year I was as good as any horseman in battalion. However, I am Jewish, and wouldn't you know, our colonel was Fritz Kuhn of the Delaware Water Gap's German Nazi Bund. I was the recipient of many none-too-sly remarks about being a Jew bastard.

"The last battalion dress formation the colonel held while I was in his battalion, my captain was absent and I had to take his place. I checked my sword, my spurs—everything was perfect. The pass in review was outstanding, until it was my turn to unsheathe my sword, salute the colonel, and take my four measured steps forward. On the third step, my spurs locked, I tripped, and I damned near skewered that Nazi bastard. Three days later, my horse and I were transferred to Fort Dix.

"After two weeks at Dix, I was sent to the firing range. My horse was a bit lame that day, so I was given one of the stable's extra horses. The exercise that day was simple. The referee calls to the equestrian to lead his horse to the starting arrow. At the sound of 'ready' the rider mounts his steed. At the sound of 'get set' the rider raises his hand. At the sound of 'go' the rider starts at a trot, drawing his .45 automatic. He then shoots twice at the target on the right, changes his horse's pace to a canter, turns to the left and fires his weapon at the target there. Then he changes the pace to a full gallop, leans forward, stands up in his stirrups, aiming his .45 forward over the horse's head at the bull's eye. Unfortunately for the horse and me, I accidentally shot his left ear off and I damn near broke my ass.

"As a consequence, here I stand in this freezing rain, on the *Queen Mary*, transferred to an antiaircraft outfit, enjoying a free ride to England. But at least I won't have a Nazi colonel as my commanding officer."

Later in the war, I received a letter from Lieutenant Greenberg. He was then a captain assigned to the First Army, with a happy first sergeant and a great company.

* * *

On the fourth day, we had a little problem on the *Queen Mary*. She was carrying the first contingent of WACs and WAVEs to be shipped overseas. They were billeted for safety on D deck, with every access protected with American MPs and British military police. The commodore of the ship had advised all officers and men that, if they were caught on D deck, they would be arrested and would spend the remainder of the voyage in his brig, positioned in the pointed bow of the ship. They would also be downgraded in rank by him, personally.

Two of my best buck sergeants, Joe Sharpe and Joe Smith, told me later that they were bored and felt that they just had to see if they could sneak up on D deck. They were having a little fun with some girls and everything was just great until an MP saw them changing cabins and sounded the alarm. Trying to hide, they immediately climbed into one of the *Mary's* large air funnels, which are air ducts. They would have been home free if Sergeant Smith hadn't lit a cigar and set off a series of smoke alarms. What a commotion! One major alarm went off that screeched we were on fire and sinking. Another tripped a series of water sprays in the commodore's office, creating one hell of a mess of his files. About fifteen MPs took the two sergeants into custody.

I didn't have any idea what had happened when I heard on the ship's intercom system, "First Sergeant Durkin to report to the commodore, posthaste on deck C, where you will meet your captain and await further orders." At about the same time, the alarms were being shut off, with repeated announcements from the commodore that we were in no danger of sinking and to "go about your duties."

Ten minutes after joining my captain, who, like me, was totally in the dark as to the problem, we were met by two very large British MPs who placed us under ship arrest. We knew it wasn't funny when two U.S. Army MP officers joined our party and called us to a loud attention. With two British MPs leading us to the commodore's quarters and the U.S. MPs bringing up our rear, I elbowed the captain and whispered, "Going to the commodore's quarters should be an honor, but this sure as hell isn't!"

The British MPs instructed us that upon entering the commodore's office we were to stand at attention, exactly two steps in front of his desk. Only the captain would report, giving his name, rank and serial number. And whatever you do, they said, "keep your frigging mouths shut, unless spoken to. Also, watch the tone of your voice." Otherwise we would wind up on bread and water for the balance of the voyage.

When we stopped two paces in front of the commodore's desk, my captain snapped his salute very sharply. The captain almost knocked his head off with his high, heavy-handed salute, which was not returned by the commodore. By the slow look he gave both of us— back and forth, back and forth—I felt as if my fly or the captain's were undone and somehow we had insulted His Royal Highness. Finally, after a couple of stony-eyed stares, he started to speak in a very cultured British accent. Never, he said, had his ship "carried the likes of you, low-browed, disgusting, blithering, bloody idiots." And then he repeated himself, which to me only meant that he did not know how to cuss.

In all fairness, he did get his points across. About then, Sergeants Sharpe and Smith were ushered into view, their hands cuffed and sheepish looks on their faces. Sharpe mugged a high shrug and a slight grin for me. We listened to the commodore dress them down, until finally, about as red-faced as anyone I have ever seen, he reached into the middle of his desk. He took out a gleaming, double-edged dagger that he must have used as a letter opener, and handed it to me, grunting loudly, "Sergeant, do your duty." I looked at my captain for direction. He just shrugged his shoulders and I thought the SOB wanted me to cut Joe's throat. So I immediately asked, "Sir, what do you want me to do with this knife?"

This really pissed him off and he just about choked when he said, "First Sergeant, I want you to remove that man's rank with that G.D. bloody dagger, at once, before I restrict your whole G.D. bloody company and intern you for the balance of this bloody war!" Then he took a deep breath and yelled, "Do you hear me?"

I not only heard him, but he was close to deafening my ears, and I was very close to losing control of my bladder. I think my captain did!

As I removed the stripes, the commodore said, "These two men will spend the balance of their voyage in my very uncomfortable brig, on bread and water, and be considered convicts by the crew of the *Mary*. So don't try any stupid Yank moves." His mean little eyes were in action again as he informed me to "step lively and accompany the MPs and the convicts to the brig, at once!"

Since the brig was in the bow of the ship, being there in heavy seas was like being enclosed in a large, windowless elevator. You shoot up very high in the air, and then you come down with one hell of a bang. You can't stand up, and with only two covers and a bolted-down cot in each cell, it was just plain hell being in there for even a few minutes. The noise was deafening; the ocean was very rough that day.

Our captain did not visit the two sergeants for the rest of the voyage. His excuse was that he did not want to meet with the commodore again. However, I spent a few hours with both Joes. The captain and I finally pieced their little adventure together and after a little detective work we realized that no real harm had been done. No marks should go against their records, especially since they were the best sergeants in our company. Therefore, as soon as we were out from under the commodore's eyes, I would hand them their stripes— with a little bit of jaw on the side.

The cells in the brig had special handholds on the walls to enable the convicts to manipulate and maneuver around their cells. The day before docking, the captain obtained permission for me to visit Sharpe and Smith. Their guards made me empty my pockets, since no food was allowed. But the British MPs were good people. They had borrowed extra food from the *Mary's* cooks for the prisoners. Although the two sergeants did not lose any weight, they did accumulate a few black marks from bouncing off their cots and walls. By the end, the British MPs and cooks idolized both Joes.

# 4

# ENGLAND

We landed in Scotland and took a train assigned for troop movements down the southeast England coast to a little town called Leek, on the Staffordshire River. My memories of Leek include taking twenty-five-mile forced hikes over its beautiful dunes, covered with late spring heather.

* * *

I remember the first mail package I received overseas. I had asked my dad to send me some new wool socks, and also include three or four pairs from my old civilian sock drawer. During the early forties, it was popular to wear red- and orange-colored wool socks to school. That first package contained two pairs of bright red wool socks. They were warm and comfortable. Consequently, I had taken the habit of wearing them while riding my bike between different gun crews near the Staffordshire River. One morning, a general's command car went past me, stopped, backed up and a brigadier general got out, staring at me. "First Sergeant, are those red socks government issue?"

I stood at attention. "Sir," my answer was, "No, sir!"

"First Sergeant, keep them off."

LEROY E. DURKIN

* * *

I have trouble remembering how we really felt during those long months in England, prior to what became the Normandy invasion. The future seemed to be an emptiness, a space. We were set up as an antiaircraft battalion protecting a B-26 medium-bomber group near Leek. It was a beautiful area of farmland and villages, but we spent most of the nights getting bombed by the Germans and returning fire. Mornings we were served our cook's breakfasts, always comprised of powdered eggs, a strip of flabby bacon, coffee or tea. On Sunday there were pancakes, and sometimes kidney stew. If we were lucky the local farmers would swap cigarettes for coffee and fresh eggs, which we boiled in our iron hats and ate as breakfast.

The German ME-109s dropped their bombs each night and the British Spitfires chased them all over the sky. Those of us on the ground were very much aware that the ammo from those machine guns up there, no matter from which country they originated, was eventually earth-bound. Air raids were scary. We were shooting cannon toward enemy ME-109 and HE-111. We were very aware of how inaccurate everyone's fire was, and how much shrapnel and explosive force was involved. Dumb luck was what we counted on.

The batteries of searchlights would pale and fan the night sky for the enemy. We would be firing our .50 calibers, 40mm, and 90mm into the night sky, knowing that what goes into the air will come down as deadly shrapnel. Our men were constantly using our "honey buckets," after near misses from ME-109 bombs and low-flying strafings.

A few of our pilots would hang out with different ground gun crews as substitutes, explaining to the top brass, if one should show up, that they were obtaining rare and valuable knowledge concerning the spread of flack at many different altitudes. Actually these pilots were merely enjoying the thrill of firing four synchronized .50 calibers on the ground. One senior pilot sitting among our antiaircraft .50 caliber ammo boxes in the revetment, asked me one day, "Why don't a couple of your senior sergeants change places with our airmen so that both

34

groups will understand what types of combat the other experiences?" Seizing the opportunity as a first sergeant, I recommended that I be invited to fly as a flack observer attached to the Eighth Air Force for twenty-four hours and accompany the colonel's B-26 planes as a replacement for his tail gunner. I think we were both a little tanked when the colonel shook my hand and said that we would have a delayed lift-off the next day at 6:30 a.m. I was there!

We were a wing of twelve B-26 bombers in groups of "wings of three," with coverage by thirty-six P-51 fighters. The colonel finished his orders that morning then turned and introduced me to the crews as a "combat first sergeant who had volunteered." He said I was replacing his tail gunner as a special flack observer. He had a few special comments to make before we boarded. It seems that the tail gunner had forgotten to deliver his parachute to the plane, so I would be considered AWOL if the plane was shot down!

The colonel directed me to stand behind his seat and hang on. The planes took off by twos, side by side, lifting with no trouble. Off in the distance some P-51 fighters could be seen moving around getting into their positions. Our plane was flying point at about 12,000 feet and I was standing behind and hanging on to the colonel's seat. It was a very interesting trip over the white cliffs of Dover and the Channel. There was a huge group of B-17s very high on our left side, shining in the morning sun. We were considerably lower. The sky over France was cloudy and as we approached the coastline the colonel was all business, sending me back to my position as the tail gunner. We pulled sharply higher over some French hills and cities, moving into and leveling off in the clouds, on our way to drop bombs over Essen.

The colonel was constantly on our intercom and communicating with our P-51s about different German flights of ME-109s, HE-111s. There was also a group of our P-38s up there assisting the P-51s in chasing the 111s and ME-109s. There is so much to see during an air mission. When we got near some cities the antiaircraft batteries were brutal. I started to earn my tail gunner's pay at about 11:30 hours. The colonel made hand signals to his wing mates. From planes roaring along a few yards below, to the side and behind him, they grinned and waved at the colonel, who had a cold corncob pipe in his mouth.

When we dropped our bombs, I was able to watch the action through the open bomb-bay doors. The doors took some shrapnel and remained wedged in an open mode, like a mortar barrage

After we made our turn at the end of our bombing run, the colonel got on the intercom and told us, to our surprise, that our primary mission that day was not the bombing, but to do a close-in series of photographs to ascertain the antiaircraft power around the city of Paris, especially the Eiffel Tower and the Aerodrome. In order to accomplish this mission, our bomb-bay doors would be opened all the way and we would fly slow and low over freight and rail yards. We were to stay alert, spotting any damage to the Eiffel Tower as well as getting an estimate of operational guns surrounding it. My job was to count any armor operational and dangerous to Allied planes.

As the colonel pulled sharply up over the Eiffel Tower my eyes were the only set of eyes in the plane looking straight out at screaming red tracer bullets. They seemed to float up toward me from the ground, but very rapidly. I was trying to count the 40mm Bofor guns, but I was much more worried that I seemed to be about fifty yards away from those damned 40mm cannon firing on automatic, along with quad .50 calibers shooting at my butt at a speed of 3,500 rounds per minute, barely missing my very wet pants.

To my relief, the colonel finally pushed the throttle and his other two wingmen banked in unison, pulling up into the bright clear blue sky where I saw our P-51 Angels. It was then that the colonel told me, "You can unstrap and come forward for some sightseeing. But we are having a little trouble with our stuck bomb bays, so the waist gunner will come back to help you use the handgrips. We don't want you to fall out, Sergeant Durkin. Remember, you don't have a parachute." As if I didn't know!

As I squirmed out of the tail gunner's hole and began to crawl up on the side of the open bomb-bay doors, I could see the Seine River falling behind like a trickle of water. I could also see one hell of a big hole in one of our wingmen's right wing. When I finally crawled up between the colonel and his co-pilot, the colonel told me to stand up and hang on to both of them. The waist gunner was taking over the tail gunner's position so that I could take in the view!

Flying over the Channel was beautiful, especially the sight of all the different planes returning to England safely. The copilot pointed out London off in the distance with all of its defensive balloons flying in the air. We approached our airfield, with all of the planes, I was told, low on fuel. Some of the planes shot red rockets, indicating wounded or dead aboard and requesting that there be medics available on landing.

While waiting our turn to land, the colonel talked about the B-26 we were flying. He thought it was a good plane, but he knew pilots who hated to fly her. The B-26 did have one big problem, he said. Her wings were too small for the loads she carried. That's why the pilots called her "The Boston Prostitute"—no visible means of support.

As our wing started to land, the colonel had his copilot radio to his wingmen to land and taxi into their "park-stat" because the colonel and his crew were going to perform a "victory roll." His copilot and waist gunner nearly had a case of borderline hysteria when the colonel shut down their communications. But he told us to stay alert because he was going to buzz the field on the deck and then the tower, going about twelve miles straight out and thirty miles back on the deck, at which point he would pull up to about 10,000 feet. From there, we would do the total victory roll.

He told me to hold tight to the back of his seat, and pulled his seat belt in as much as he could to help me. Throughout the distance to his twelve-mile marker the colonel was diving the plane, trying to perform a victory roll until it looked like we were at the same height off the ground as two British telephone poles we passed. The co-pilot was a very young second lieutenant and this was his first flight with the colonel. I felt sorry for him. He was praying and begging the colonel to reconsider because this was a "f****** Boston Prostitute," it simply wasn't capable of doing a victory roll. The colonel just laughed and kept pointing to a big brass plate on the control panel that said, "Do not roll."

As we started back to the twenty-mile marker, the colonel said that if the kid didn't shut the hell up he was going to let me change places with him and I could land the plane. Of course I knew he would never do that, but. The lieutenant now just about wanted to jump! As we arrived at the twenty-mile marker the colonel pulled back on the stick and went about ten to twenty miles further, climbing at full throttle, reaching for elevation. When the plane started doing a "shimmer-shake," I yelled to the colonel above the roar. He pointed down as he lined up on the left side over the base and told us to hang on for a real first! He started a wing-over as the start of a "victory roll." However, the wing-over did not carry the plane's weight and we started a gigantic "side slip" into a possible tailspin, and it took all of their strength to pull the "Boston Prostitute" up to a level flight just a few yards higher than a large tree. I'll be damned if the colonel didn't climb back up and try to do a wing-over from the right side. But this time I think he chickened out. We came in for a perfect landing, with a thimbleful of fuel and a very smelly cockpit. I was back on the ground—without a chute, the only way I was going to get there alive.

As we were getting out of the plane, the colonel laughingly advised me that this had been his last flight. He would now be wearing a single star as a brigadier general, and flying a desk. I took two steps back, and gave him his first "high ball" as a general, damn near falling out of the plane's door as I did it. The general then informed his copilot that he was now a captain and in charge of this "Boston Prostitute"—"with a visible means of support, kid, and don't you forget it!"

* * *

Rumors were plentiful. All the signs pointed to an imminent invasion of Europe when we were given what turned out to be our last pass to London. I had no trouble obtaining forty-eight-hour passes for my best noncom, Sergeant Joe Smith, and our mentor, First Lieutenant Viola.

Lieutenant Viola had led my inspection of Sergeant Joe's guns, tracks, and equipment. His weapons were cosmolined where needed to protect them from the saltwater spray during the trip across the English Channel. We were definitely going to be armed for instant combat duty even before we reached the Channel. In case of air raids, Joe's tracks had to be combat ready fore and aft aboard ship—

protection from possible strafing runs of enemy planes. The inspection went well. The equipment was ready.

Our train into London was jammed with men in uniforms. We shot the bull with the Coast Guard, Navy, Canadian troops, FFI (Free French) and Free Polish—all champing at the bit, as we were, and ready to go. But first we were going to enjoy our time in London.

The bars, pubs, and hotel bars we spent our time in were packed with MPs and brass, British as well as American. The last one we sat in for quite a while, but it was obvious Lieutenant Viola was tired of the noise. He was on his third letter to his wife, telling her over and over again that we would cover his back, and Joe and I would not let him do anything stupid, and he loved her, etc., etc. Finally he decided he was returning to camp on the next train, making Sergeant Joe and me promise before he left we would not get into trouble.

Within fifteen minutes, my nerves were raw from Sergeant Joe's constant and very loud complaining, about everything and anything. Then he swore I'd forgotten how to hold an intelligent conversation and said, "It's impossible for you to stroll. You strut like a numby first sergeant on parade, and unless you tone it down, even my charming manners and handsome face won't be enough to attract a girl that is not a bow-wow!"

Finally he ran out of steam. By now we were standing in front of the USO on Piccadilly Square. We were hungry and agreed that at least we could relax a little with free doughnuts and hot chocolate, maybe shoot a little pool and play a few games of ping pong. "Who knows, Joe," I said. "You might even meet a girl with a personality like that Georgia peach you nearly married during our basic training. The one that looked a little like a monkey. Perhaps you may even hold a brief conversation, maybe not very intelligent, but it will surely be our last opportunity for one hell of a long time."

Joe and I were surprised to find Lieutenant Viola having his third doughnut and second cup of coffee with another second lieutenant with whom he had been a classmate at Penn State. We shot the breeze for a while, then agreed to meet on the train for Leek on the Staff later. Sergeant Joe and I took a short tour through the USO. I wanted to

39

write a letter home to my dad. Joe got both misty homesick and pissed off about the doggone war and his girl back home. Most of all he worried about "that SOB draft dodger who was probably making out with his girl every night and whispering in her ear."

I pointed out that he had been trying for months to do the same things to the cute British girls in England. Joe started to hiccup, one sure sign he was upset. I remember I looked into Joe's tear-streaked face, and as I rested my chin on my fist, I murmured to him, "Please, shut the hell up. You're not only weird, you're getting on people's nerves. Everyone in here is shushing you." Joe wiped his eyes, blew his nose, went into the men's room, and came out saying he was ready for more coffee and doughnuts. Of course the coffee, in Joe's words, was "like love in a canoe, f***ing near water," and the doughnuts were not tasty, which really pissed him off again.

About then, trying to get him to stop complaining, I suggested we check out the girl at the front desk. We both agreed that the young receptionist was pretty enough for Joe to cuddle up to and forget his "two-timing girlfriend and her draft-dodging son of an ape" back in the States. We approached the desk of a very attractive young lady who turned out to be condescending and very unhappy. She managed to tell us off, holding us responsible for her boyfriend being in Africa fighting Rommel. "There were too many damned Yanks in her country," she said, "who thought they were the saviors of the world." And glad she would be when we were all gone and her Clive was returned to dear old England. It was a very awkward moment. Then, glaring at Joe, she upset her coffee on her desk and Joe's pant leg and got *really* pissed off

For a few seconds Joe shuffled about uneasily. Then, incredibly, looking her straight in the eye, he blurted out, "How about girls? How does a guy get some action around here? What are all of the girls, queer? When was the last time you were serviced by a real good Yankee man?"

To her credit, she accepted Joe's question as though he had asked for the time of day. She watched us leave without saying a word, but I guess her Clive must have been in Italy by then because she gave

Joe a beautiful "Italian salute," the middle finger of her right hand totally extended. We went through the doors, down the steps, and I yelled at Joe, "You stupid bastard. She could have called the MPs. Then we would really have been in deep shit!" It was useless. Joe was grinning and beamed at me with real satisfaction. Finally, I had to laugh. He was as happy as a puppy that had just peed on a new rug and gotten away with it.

We watched the Bobbies and MPs chasing soldiers and sailors down into the subways because of a heavy German air raid. Then we met Lieutenant Viola at 7 p.m. and returned to Leek on the Staff, the village near Southampton where we were camped.

\* \* \*

We had been using emergency quarters for three days and nights in the Southampton area. The battalion was bedded down in old, worn-out pyramidal tents, and the weather matched the tents. They were both nasty, raining and leaking until everything to some degree was wet. Joe and I finally agreed that we should sneak under the fence and try for the nearest pub and a couple of tankards of good English stout.

Reaching the pub was very good combat training—crawling, slipping around corners, buildings, etc. without being picked up by British or American MPs. When we were finally belly-up to the very crowded bar we were surrounded by very rough-looking British and Canadian combat soldiers. It looked like Joe and I were the only two Americans in the building, and we quietly agreed that it was going to be one hell of a job getting back to "safe quarters."

While pondering this problem, Joe nudged me with his elbow. We weren't the only Americans. Two of our men were trying to hide from us at the back end of the bar. Now these two "rara avis" (rare birds) were considered to be the biggest "f****-ups" in this man's army. They had both been in the stockade during basic in Georgia, picked up in New York for being AWOL, quarantined for hitting a second lieutenant and in general had been a constant problem. They were inseparable. Private Lane was about five feet four inches and his buddy, PFC Gibbons, was six feet four inches. Gibbons was rumored to have connections to the mob, as a former enforcer and collector for a Bronx "family." He was a reputed breaker of arms and elbows and one nasty SOB. During training, I had seen Gibbons pick up an air-cooled .50 caliber machine gun and fire it at moving targets from the hips. It was one hell of a performance, and he didn't stagger.

Lane and Gibbons were certainly a very good pair to give a wide berth. Needless to say they were both nasty drunks, and Lane, being the smallest, was the meanest. He would constantly leer at girls in a bar, even if they were with someone, knowing full well that Gibbons could handle three or four average brutes at a time. With this in mind, I nervously pointed out to Sergeant Joe that we were the only Yanks in the bar, and we numbered four. The rest were British combat soldiers—the tough kind, the ones home on combat leave, the dangerous type with killing ability! Lane and Gibbons had obviously been drinking in the pub at least a couple of hours prior to our arrival and Lane was already displaying his mean streak. He would soon pick a fight with some Britishers and we would all get the hell kicked out of us and be escorted back to base under arrest by both U.S. and British MPs. It was a no-win situation. *Good-bye stripes*, I thought.

Joe and I had just finished our second tankard of stout when I saw Lane put down his tankard, clear his throat, reach up with his right hand, and punch a British staff sergeant who was towering over him. He was an obvious combat warrior and he yelled so loud that the total pub was suddenly deathly quiet. Then Lane took a deep breath and started to yell, "F*** the King." The total pub heard the idiot. The British soldier, who was very well tanked, looked down at Lane and in a stentorian voice said: "Hi say—you caunt do that, you know. You caunt *approach* 'im."

It took a little time for everyone in the pub to understand exactly what the British staff sergeant's answer had been to Lane. When we did, to a man, we all raised our glasses and drank a toast to the King's health. Then the pub owner, alerted that we were going to France in a very few days, instructed his bartenders to fill everyone's tankards. The drinks were on the house, and the next drink would be a toast to

42

President Roosevelt. Then we honored Eisenhower, then Churchill, then Eisenhower again. Along the way we picked up some very happy singers. Lane was sitting on the bar with his arm around a Cockney soldier who was drunk as a skunk and trying to teach him an old British/ Scottish army barracks song. The pub owner's wife was sober enough to write the words down for me:

*Oh, the dogs they had a meeting*
*They came from near and far*
*And some dogs came by motorbus*
*And some by motor car*
*On entering the meeting hall*
*Each dog would take a look*
*Where he had to hang his arshole*
*Up high upon a hook.*

*Now when they were assembled,*
*Each canine son and sire.*
*Some dirty bull— son of a bitch*
*Jumped up and hollered fire.*
*Now all was in a panic*
*T'was hell upon to look*
*Each doggie grabbed at random*
*An arshole from a hook*

*The arsholes were all mixed up*
*Which made each doggie sore,*
*To have to wear another dog's ars*
*He'd never worn before.*
*And that is why to this day*
*A dog will leave a bone*
*To run and smell another dog's ars*
*To see if it's his own!*

After our narrow escape from having the hell beat out of us, we went crawling on our bellies under the outer ring of barbed-wire fence, back to our tents. The trip through the mud was child's play. The next afternoon we were assigned to a ship and promptly loaded aboard. Next stop, Normandy, France!

# 5

# D-DAY

The great day had come! Through the night hours of June 5 and 6, 1944, the mightiest fleet the world had ever known was on its way to begin the liberation of Europe. More than 4,000 ships were en route from England to the coast of France. Aboard was the vanguard of armies that were to swell to more than 4 million men. Above was a mighty air armada of more than 3,000 warplanes.

In his final words to his troops, General Eisenhower told us, "If our fighting is as good as our training, God help the Nazis. My deep appreciation to each of you for duty well performed in the past and with best of luck for the future!" Our battalion had heard this at dusk on June 1, while standing along with two other battalions at full attention in a downpour.

Although we were not supposed to know the "jump-off time," it was difficult to keep this type of information from the hard-core sergeants as we got close to the general's new and final choice of zero hour, early in the morning on Monday June 5. That day, however, began with heavy winds and high seas. This would have taken too great a toll of the landing forces, so the operation was postponed. All day Monday the Channel was rough. Just standing on the wharf's planking made many soldiers sick, which, in turn, made other soldiers anxious and sick. Some assault-force ships that had already put to sea had to return to port with their complements of hundreds of tensed-up, action-eager troops. The rest of us just waited—impatient, tired, and underfed.

Monday night, the weather was still bad although it had moderated somewhat. But General Eisenhower flashed the signal. In the harbors thousands of vessels from battleships to assault boats and PT boats sounded their battle stations. With soldiers crowded aboard troopships and landing crafts, the fleet headed out to sea. The faces of the men reflected every possible facet of human emotion. We were going into battle in a country most of us had never seen before. Many of us would see action for the first time. Dice and card games flourished, with jeep hoods as tables and invasion money as stakes. Some sang, many prayed, and most of us just stood with a buddy and wondered what tomorrow would bring. Rumors had it that casualties on the beach would run twenty to thirty percent. Hell, General Eisenhower's speech estimated that casualties in the 101st and 82nd Airborne Divisions could be as high as forty percent. I remember looking at my men and wondering "Who will I lose?"

There were more than 2.8 million men in the Allied Expeditionary Force, but only a few thousand were leading the way in the landings. Around 2 a.m. on the morning of June 6 we were about six miles from the French coast. Our battalion was aboard LCVPs (landing craft vehicle personnel), one of the larger transports we used to cross the Channel. We spent the first day with our half-tracks combat-lined on the deck with our four .50 caliber guns, protecting different troop LCVPs. So we were not off-loaded for thirty-six hours. The Allied Air Forces had shifted most of its bombing to "daylight pinpoint," leaving nighttime to the thinned-out enemy. That meant that the night-flying German bombers, which were too high for us to reach, would drop bombs blindly, hoping that they would get lucky and hit some landing craft. We were straddled by bombs a few times before we received our orders to off-load.

The water was very choppy and every one of us was nervous. We just hoped we would not slip, fall into the water, and join the many, many bodies floating there. Many of us were not so much afraid as we were tense, after all the days and nights of waiting for D-Day to arrive and our great adventure to begin. As the small ships and LCVPs loaded up and pulled away from the larger ships and transports, they began to rock and pitch. Waves began slapping at the sides and bows of the boats, sending icy cold spray flying through the air. Before long everyone was soaked to the skin.

\* \* \*

The first waves of the invasion had been the assault soldiers, all under mortar and machine-gun fire from the enemy. Each LCVP carried thirty-two men and each thirty-two-man section was a team in the attack. A typical boat had a boat section leader standing in the bow, a second lieutenant armed with a .45 caliber side arm and a carbine. Just behind him stood five riflemen carrying semi-automatic Garand rifles (M-1s). Each of these men had ninety-six extra rounds in clips of eight. The clips were in pouches on the wide web belt worn around their waists. Tied to the suspenders that helped support the belts were five hand grenades and four smoke grenades. Every second soldier also carried a half-pound of TNT plus the fuse to explode it.

Next came four men, also armed with M-1s, who made up a special wire-cutting team. Their very hazardous job was to open gaps through barbed wire with the big cutter they carried. Behind this team were two Browning automatic rifle teams, each with six men. A BAR, as the gun is called, is more like a machine gun than a rifle. It sprays lead around in rapid fire. Each team carried 900 rounds of ammunition.

After them came two men with bazookas, the weird weapon that looks like a length of stovepipe and fires a small bomb-like rocket. The range is only a few hundred yards, but when it hits, the rocket explodes with great force and can bum its way through the thin steel plate of a half-track. Each bazooka man had an assistant to load the barrel and carry the extra rockets. The assistant was armed with a carbine.

The next four men made up a light mortar team. They carried a 60mm mortar whose barrel was slightly more than two and half inches wide, plus twenty mortar shells. Most of us thought the mortar was the

47

infantry's most effective weapon. It is a tubular gun that lobs its shell high into the air so that it can reach over walls, hills and hedgerows. The firing is accurate, and when the shell explodes it shatters into thousands of sharp fragments, wounding or killing anything in the immediate area.

Finally, there was a flamethrower team of two men. Their flamethrower spurted slightly jellied gasoline through the air. It was set on fire as it left the nozzle and burned furiously for some short time after it hit. The flamethrowers were to be used against concrete pillboxes and German gun emplacements. These teams were supposed to spray a pillbox with burning jelly, to keep the enemy inside from shooting at our soldiers until the fire burned out.

\* \* \*

The first three or four hours of the assault would answer an awesome question: "Could the assault sections break through Hitler's Atlantic Wall?" The enormous weight of the whole gigantic effort rested entirely, for the time being, on those thirty-two-men sections in the LCVPs. What they needed most was courage, and courage was something that could not be issued like helmets or hand grenades. In fact, courage is a most mysterious quality. Every one of us feared that we did not have enough courage. Many did not, because they already secretly felt that we were not going to be able to cross the beach and live through the hellish German gunfire.

By 7 a.m. no one had advanced beyond the beach because the five roads leading from it were still held by the enemy, and their machine guns and 80mm cannon were growing hotter by the second. A good many of the enemy had recovered from the preliminary bombing from our aircraft and the shelling by our warships. The initial shock had worn off. Their artillery and mortar shells were pounding the flat beaches. Machine guns and automatic rifles sprayed fire across the open spaces. Snipers aiming from the hills were picking off individual soldiers, both wounded and able ones. Most of the survivors of the first and second waves had scattered along the dunes and had forgotten about attacking. Their only thoughts were to stay alive.

Three boats in the second wave were receiving very strong mortar and machine-gun fire. One boat grounded seventy-five yards offshore. As its ramp came down, machine-gun fire beat a tattoo on the bow. The captain got about ten yards through the water before he was hit twice in the leg and shoulder. "I'm hit, I'm hit," he yelled. "Try to make it in," shouted a medic at the front, who was standing on the boat's ramp; but the captain slumped down and disappeared into the waves. The medic jumped in after him and was shot and killed before he could get to where the captain had vanished. Every member of that boat section, except one, was killed or wounded before reaching the beach.

The tide was coming in very fast. It advanced at the rate of eight feet in the half hour from 7:00 a.m. to 7:30 a.m. It was beginning to wash up a line of dead soldiers along with wrecked pieces of equipment, especially hundreds of inflated twin-tube life preservers. Many of the wounded, unable to crawl faster than the tides progressed, had drowned in the surge of the surf. It was a terrible time in which men, driven out of their wits, did desperate, strange things.

One wounded man, partway across the sands, was hiding behind and actually hugging an active mine, too scared to release his hold. Most of the soldiers were in a state of shock like people that have been in a terrible accident. They were dazed, numb. Many of them could not move at all. They realized they were too stunned to act. A freezing cold surf, severe cases of seasickness, and the horror of seeing their buddies shot down or blown to pieces allied to their inability to move. It seemed impossible that the attack could ever move forward again. Back in the boats, we asked: Would the first couple of waves break through the beach and Hitler's Atlantic Wall? We needed their courage to get us a toehold on the beach coast. Everything depended on the men in those first waves—*everything.*

It made no difference how many units of men were waiting off the beach on the LCTs or LCVPs. It was imperative that the five roads be taken from the Germans as soon as possible. Hundreds of thousands of men were waiting for this. They would follow with millions of tons of desperately needed supplies, not only for the men of the first waves who were still alive, but for the fighting divisions that would follow them.

Due to their lack of momentum, the horrors they had witnessed, and the many snipers firing from the hills, quite a few common soldiers took it upon themselves, without orders, to try to do something. Any action, they felt, was better than none. Each man acted alone. It was the courage and bravery of the common soldier that restarted the assault. By nightfall, we had our toehold in the Omaha Beach area. It was only a mile and a half deep at its deepest, which was in the center near the village of Collaville. Omaha cost a lot. About 2,000 men were dead, wounded or missing.

But we were only a couple of miles short of Caen, and Caen was only 150 miles from Paris. The country was all flat and perfect for our tanks and half-tracks. However, due to the hedgerows and the fierce fighting, it took us seven weeks until July 25 to break out by way of St. Lo and head for Paris. Throughout June, no urging was necessary to make us dig in. Night and day we were pounded by German mortar fire.

Whenever possible, the men cleaned their weapons, dug new, more elaborate, safer foxholes. Those who had been sleeping in the open were now under cover again. Due to severe rain all of the second and third day, we became fully aware of the difference between French mud puddles and what we remembered of plain old mud. Occasionally, an ambulance would drive by and ask if our half-track was in need of aspirin, gauze, or sulphur powder for breaks in the skin, athlete's foot, and earaches. They might also have the latest *Stars and Stripes*.

Writing this book has brought back many memories of the firefights fought mainly on the back roads leading toward potential ambushes, snipers, or a small skirmish.

Different soldiers may very well have different recollections of the same firefight—how long it lasted, how fierce the fighting was. When you are in one, you tend to lose all trace of time. You remember in successive stages of shock your fear and anger when a buddy falls, but your mind hates to accept all of it. When you remember war, you tend not to recall the brutal actions. Your mind tries to erase the noise, the loss of good men, the horrible apprehension you always felt.

You know a hell of a lot happened but, thanks to God, your memory can't grasp or recall all of those images. Subconsciously your mind erases some portions from your memory bank, in order to protect your sanity. So what I remember most of all is Joe swearing at me and I occasionally busting his balls. We learned as soldiers, during basic training, to pair up as buddies and to cover each other's back in combat pairs.

* * *

A few days after landing, it was raining again. So far we had been unable to join up with the balance of our battalion, currently somewhere down the road and probably lost. The rain was now a drenching storm and the water was sluicing so hard the drivers could not see a track's length in front of them. The ruts in the road were a foot wide and eight to ten inches deep. During flashes of lightning, the hedgerows we saw all looked alike, all very dangerous. It was kind of like tiptoeing through a very wet hell.

As we moved along, we saw an occasional burned-out truck or a tank rusted and abandoned, but there was still no sight or sound of any of the rest of our battalion. We came across one German tank that had been bombed and burned, and three members of our graves detail put two German cadavers they had removed from the tank into body bags. They told me that every dead German they interred was given a military burial.

We knew the Germans were on the other side of the hedgerows. So I decided to circle our half-tracks, post guards, and feed the men their rations. I thought hot coffee and C rations would give then a welcome respite before we wandered into enemy territory. We used our trenching shovels to dig down about two and a half feet until we hit relatively dry gravel. Then we put some branches across the trench we had dug, removed the tarpaulin from our truck, and spread it over our hole as a roof. There was room enough in the hole for our equipment and six or seven men.

I posted a rotating armed guard. When not on guard duty, the men played a little poker by flashlights until dark. Worn out, most of us fell asleep at once. At about 11 p.m. by my army watch, Corporal Woods, our truck driver, whispered that he had to pee and began crawling out from under our cover. I told *him* to take a few steps away from our covering and to try to be quiet about it. A couple of minutes later Woods whispered, "Hey, Sarge, you ought to see these big French mosquitoes. They are really big and they light up like fireflies."

I crawled out to relieve myself and yelled at Woods, "You stupid jackass. Those fireflies are tracers being fired by very unfriendly Nazis trying to shoot down our planes. And what goes up, comes down as shrapnel."

At this point, a voice on the other side of the hedgerow asked quite loudly, "What's the password?"

I said, "We don't have a password for tonight because we have not hooked up with our battalion to receive our password." We then heard three shots—pow-pow-pow—that seemed to be coming through the hedgerow in front of us, scaring poor Woods so badly he messed his pants.

At dawn, the rain stopped and as the light increased we could see that we had been parked about fifty yards from a bombed-out railroad yard and a detour manned by a military police platoon. They told me that our battalion had used the detour and should be in the vicinity of Ste. Mere Eglise. One of them led me to the crossroads that were still wet and very muddy. He wanted to make sure that the road signs were pointing in the correct direction, and warned me that the Germans were reversing the signs.

As we stood at the cross roads, I noted that the MP was standing on a large manhole-cover-like lid. We were both stamping on the lid to rid the mud from our boots. In fact the MP was actually doing a pretty good tap dance when I asked if all of the cross roads were supplied with these manhole covers. He laughed. It seems we were knocking the mud off our boots by stamping on a live German tank mine. I must have had a look of abject terror on my face, because he laughed again and said that his platoon had been using this mine to keep their feet dry and warm while they directed traffic for half of the Third Army. What's more, he said that General Patton had danced a jig on the mine and told him it was "great fun." "BS, sir," he said he—in army parlance—"muttered but not uttered. "

\* \* \*

I left Sergeant Smith, who was zeroing in his half-track's four .50 calibers near the church in Ste. Mere Eglise, with an order that he try to locate the whereabouts of Company D's headquarters and if possible our captain. One of the MPs was being used as a motorcycle dispatch rider and he was sitting astride his motorcycle with his feet in two mud puddles, one on each side. When I saw a sign indicating that a command post was nearby, he pointed and said, "Follow that jeep to the other side of that orchard. They can help you."

It was one hell of a relief to see one of our jeeps, even though its rear axle was broken and it was totally out of action. Then I saw our captain, obviously harassed and standing on the hood of his jeep, peering into the mist looking for his lost company and his first sergeant. Instead of rewarding me with a cup of hot coffee, he yelled, "Where in the hell have you been?" He chewed out my butt for jeopardizing his career. He tried to make me believe that as the first sergeant I was responsible for all of Company D's equipment—weapons, the cooks, truck drivers—everything, including the frigging jeep he was standing on.

The Germans held the area on the outer perimeters of Ste. Mere Eglise. Small fields and large impenetrable hedgerows separated us from them. The Germans and their mortars were on the other side of those hedges, hoping for a lucky shot over them. The roads were full of motion in both directions. The bivouac areas were busy laying telephone wires, which the enemy busily tore up. Officers and sergeants were constantly asking strangers to help find their men, jeeps, trucks, areas, etc. The mortars were interrupted by an occasional sniper's deadly fire. The snap-bang of a sniper's near miss guaranteed the soiling of somebody' s underwear.

The proximity of the enemy to our men created the occasional whirling of shrapnel, and shortly after a yell for a medic. The mortar is the infantry's personal artillery. It has a short barrel with no taper and looks like a three- or four-foot length of stove pipe. This barrel stands on the ground locked into a thick metal plate about the size of a small luncheon tabletop. A pair of folding legs holds the front of the barrel so that the barrel is slanted up at a sharp angle to its base plate, standing the barrel almost vertical. The mortar is not loaded through a breach like a rifle or a cannon. There is no breach; and the bottom end of the barrel is closed. A soldier loads and fires at the same time, by dropping the shell down the muzzle. When dropped down into the muzzle the firing charge explodes when the shell hits the bottom of the tube and instantly it comes back up and out of the tube with a very loud bang and a tremendous whir as the round pushes the air ahead of it. The shell then proceeds up into the air in a great noisy arc, going very high and dropping with an enormous whiz-bang within 100 to 110 yards of its perimeter.

It was scary—very, very scary. There were noisy mortar rounds coming in and going out. Behind our area a Caterpillar bulldozer was trying to drag a tank destroyer out of a ditch, attracting a hell of a lot of mortar fire from the other side of the hedgerows. What a mess!

Mortar and sniper fire from over the hedgerows took a terrible toll. We already had one of the biggest emergency cemeteries and an ammunition dump loaded with unused body bags. Most of the men talked about the number of body bags in very low voices, knowing the bags had a very large appetite.

The colonel had loaned his command car to the general, hoping it would give him a few points or a transfer to a better command, but that was wishful thinking. The general had never been known to repay any overdue favors. That morning the colonel was heard to state vehemently, "The general's a stupid SOB," not loudly, but softly spoken, with class, to his driver.

Like all command cars in a combat area, it was fitted with a big black radio sending set on the back seat. Its aerial was a willowing rod which stuck out beyond the rear seat and banged against every tree

54

the cab went under, thoroughly pissing off the driver and the general. The radio operator cussed the driver constantly and accused him of running under trees with the sole purpose of busting his hump. Of course, this always resulted in a dressing down of both driver and operator.

Unfortunately, after a sharp swerve by the driver avoiding (he claimed) a deep hole left by a mortar round, about six feet of the aerial snapped off. The radio would no longer receive or transmit, making the operator so pissed off that he would not speak to the driver for the next twenty-four hours.

The next thing that happened in the command car was the general losing his balance while going around a curve at about thirty-five miles an hour and falling out. Fortunately for him, he landed in a huge pile of cow dung that had been heaped against the brick wall of an old barn. Due to the heavy rains over the past few weeks, the manure was extremely slippery and odious. The driver stopped the car, ran over to the general and started to try to brush some of the dung from his uniform. He was laughing like a jackass, at which point the general scared the hell out of him by drawing his .45 side arm and firing it just over his head at a German ME-109 that was strafing about two miles distant and way out of range. The gun had only been twelve inches from the driver's ear. Once underway this enabled his driver to fake a deaf ear to the point that he would turn left when the general ordered him to turn right. They were damn near captured by a lost German patrol that was more scared than the general.

* * *

A blanket order was issued from SHAEF. All Allied airplanes flying over the beach would leave their wheels down, so that antiaircraft would be free to shoot at all aircraft with their wheels up. If the wheels were *not* down they were the enemy, and therein lies a story.

It seems that a Canadian Hurricane had been hit in the hydraulic system over Paris. It just made it back to Omaha Beach, but its wheels could not be lowered. I remember standing by Sergeant Smith, drawing my .45 side arm. It was probably a captured British plane, we agreed, maybe trying to get a few free strafing runs over us and possibly sink one of our off-loading ships at the beach. Without warning Sergeant Smith's half-track's four .50 calibers opened up, scaring the hell out of us. Corporal McGonigal was doing the shooting and by stupid luck the tracers hit the plane a number of times.

The pilot began to do a dead stick into the Channel, filling his scoop and bringing the plane to a slow sinking in the shore surf. Then a very pissed-off Canadian pilot popped his canopy and waded in off the beach. "Prior to identifying my plane you stupid bastards at least someone on this beach should know the difference between a Hurricane and an ME-109!" And once he established himself as a true Canadian pilot he wanted to shoot the SOB that didn't like Canadians. Corporal McGonigal wasn't found until the next day in a small café in Ste. Mere Eglise, drunk and swearing like everyone else that no one had fired even one round, let alone a hit. Corporal McGonigal swore up and down that he did not fire at the Canadian, so how could he hit the plane, especially when the Canadian pilot stated that his plane cost over $600,000 and threatened a monumental kick in the ass to the perpetrator.

Corporal McGonigal continued to swear on his grandmother's poor soul that he did not shoot nor did he fire at the Canadian. Not until he was on the *Zanesville Victory* on the way home did he finally insist that his aim was perfectly true during that small episode at Normandy.

# 6

# FROM ST. LO TO PARIS

Nine-tenths of a war is waiting around impatiently for the other one-tenth to happen. During our month and a half in the hedgerows under mortar and sniper fire we learned the meaning of combat awareness, caution and the frenzy of positive engagement. But most of all we were aware that we were blessed by our individual guardian angels.

The weather was perfect the day we were alerted by headquarters that we should be moving on Paris within three or four days. I had to alert all half-tracks for combat via call signs and routes; with Sergeant Smith as my backup I needed someone to help cover my back, because the hike between the different tracks was extremely hazardous. That was especially true of the tracks through a couple of large fields that had been rebuilt and reoriented by combat engineers to allow our fighter planes to land and take off from France instead of England. There was still German artillery at the far end of the makeshift runway, making it necessary for planes to make a hard right-turn bank and achieve altitude quickly for a safe takeoff and landing.

Having decided to take a shortcut across the fields to save some time, Sergeant Joe and I were stalking through it Indian style, very cautiously. Suddenly, we noticed a couple of American pilots taking an early morning hike in our direction, as though they didn't have a care in the world. They were practice flying with their hands. As we approached them I murmured to Joe that I intended to alert these flyboys, even though they both were carrying their .45 caliber guns in their shoulder holsters, that they should not go near any hedgerows or heavy bushes. There might be snipers there who would gladly receive an Iron Cross for killing two hotshot pilots. Sergeant Joe said, "Right, good idea. They have it tough enough just having to fly their P-47s."

When we got close enough to warn them, the bigger of the two pilots started yelling and flapping his arms. He started to jump up and down and said, "I'll be damned. That's him. It's Durk. That's my buddy, that's Durk, the best." By now I realized that the big guy was Marty Garton from Millville, a schoolmate from my grammar and high school basketball-baseball days. I hadn't seen Marty since he received a football scholarship to the University of Arkansas.

Marty lifted me up off my feet, weapons and all, in a real bear hug, tears running down his cheek. "I love ya, Durk," he said. "I haven't seen any of the old gang since leaving home. Remember our trips, hitchhiking to the Steel Pier in Atlantic City, standing in the ballroom while we heard the songs over and over till we could learn the words and sing them all the way home? Remember the song 'I Don't Want to Set the World On Fire' and how we couldn't catch a ride and we walked singing as loud as we could, and you took your shoes off and walked barefoot, your shoes around your neck until Speed Meilly and I carried you almost into Vineland, until that old truck gave us a ride to the diner in South Millville? Didn't we have some great times?"

Finally, Marty apologized for his poor manners and introduced his wingman, a second lieutenant whose call sign was "A-1" so his nickname was A-one. Right away A-one and Sergeant Joe hit it off. Sergeant Joe had his side arm .45 and a German Luger in a shoulder holster. A-one had his .45 as a shoulder holster, and carried his German Luger on the hip. They both started shooting at a crashed P-38 at the end of our field. The P-38 had been riddled and belly-crashed during the invasion.

They were like two kids playing at war. Marty explained why he outranked A-one. It seems he had shot down four enemy planes plus one possible. A-one claimed two enemy and one possible, but he was optimistic. While we talked, A-one steered us over to their flight line and their planes. Marty's had a painting on his cowling of a rooster whose head was a hatchet with one eye, with the plane's name, "The Chopper," below. I was invited on board with Marty. Joe and A-one got into his Wildcat. Marty, still the red ass of our youth, tried to convince me I could fly, offering to start up the big engine. "The Chopper will fly all by itself," he said. At this point, needless to say I began to haul ass out of The Chopper, well aware that Marty might laughingly really turn over the engine and I'd be nutty enough to taxi a few feet and accidentally take off.

After shooting the bull, we walked back to their kitchen for coffee and listened to Marty try to con the cook out of a large can of pineapple, always his favorite snack. The cook gave us a single can with four spoons. Early July in Normandy is well-known for its yellow jackets that sting and invade picnics. I'll never forget the bellow from A-one when he put a piece of pineapple in his mouth that was covered with several very pissed-off yellow jackets. They stung him royally, causing Joe to mount an aggressive attack with his beat-up Philadelphia Phillies cap on a very angry bunch of yellow jackets.

Changing the subject, I told them, "Rumor has it we will be moving within the week to liberate Paris. But we'll be here tomorrow for sure and I'll ask the cooks to make a special pineapple cake for your return from your mission." As Marty and A-one's group lifted off at 7:15 a.m. the next morning, Joe and I with a few buddies were there to wish them bon voyage. They were due back around 11:30 and we had a big crowd waiting for them. When the planes landed and parked, A-one nearly fell out of his cockpit. He rolled off the wing and threw his helmet and goggles on the ground and came over and grabbed me. He was so emotional he could hardly speak. The tears were rolling down his cheeks as he cried, "Marty went in."

The B-17s Marty and A-one were protecting were jumped going to their target and again on their way back. Two fresh German flights of 109s were waiting for Marty's group. A-one was flying on fumes and Marty told him, "Break off your fight and head home as fast as possible," he said The Chopper had sufficient fuel to take on the two ME-109s and he did. When A-one looked back he saw one ME-109 was afire and Marty was also going in—straight into the marshland on the west side of Paris.

*First Lieutenant Marty Garton AAF Fighter*
*Squadron Killed in Action*
*1921–1944*

*"Bravery is the capacity to perform nobly even when*
*scared half to death"*
*—Unknown*

\* \* \*

We were damned tired of it. Every time we tried to move down the road we had to take full clips, ready to repel any enemy at the hedgerows. We all carried rifles, carbines or automatics. Due to the constant rain and mud, the men who carried rifles put condoms on the end of their weapons to keep dirt from getting into the muzzles. Everywhere on the roads there were minor accidents that harassed the combat MPs. Due to poor drainage in the ditches, the water seemed to get deeper by the hour. Finally, in early July, the rainy season seemed to be over. Our phone wires were pretty well tied into other companies, platoons, squads, etc.

It was a typical summer day in France when a call came into headquarters that I was needed at half-track number 3. Sergeant Gargano's track was near the bombed church on the square, about one and a half kilometers beyond number 3's field of fire. It was one hell of a lonely walk for me because of the proximity to the hedgerows and snipers. I had to walk as close to the hedgerows as possible and to stay in touch with the combat MPs, so that they could cover my butt.

German snipers were very active in the Ste. Mere Eglise sector. As I approached number 3's outpost and their security guard, I was approximately fifty yards from their track. Having tapped into the

60

telephone wire, the guard was able to announce my approach to the track's area of control. Due to the lack of ground cover, I got there by "Indian crawling," as we called it—belly on the grass and butt in the air, moving as fast as possible—and then did the last twelve to fifteen yards using an "army crawl," finally rising up and rolling into the revetment.

Sergeant Gargano, the track commander, indicated that I was to call our captain for further instructions. He asked if I could use his forward observer's phone to make the call. Later, I mentally kicked my butt for not being more observant. The entire crew in the revetment was bellied down and to a man had their M-1 rifles zeroed in on the church's belfry. I just didn't notice it at the time, so I made myself comfortable, totally exposed to the church, picked up the phone's case and began to crank the telephone. Just as I started to twist my body to get even more comfortable, I was rewarded by a loud crack, very similar to the crack of summer lightning when it hits a tree and the slap. Then there was a loud "zingggg" of a round as it hit the steel backrest of the forward observer's seat.

Not only had I nearly been hit by a sniper, one of the crew's return rifle fire barely missed my head when he pulled off a full clip aimed into the church's steeple. I was pissed off Gargano and his crew had set me up as bait for the sniper, maybe in hopes that they could get a medal for killing the sniper who shot their wonderful first sergeant. The crew was very apologetic, but they couldn't control their stupid giggles. It took all my self-control not to pull out my .45 and blow Sergeant Gargano a new rectum.

When I called the command post and told Lieutenant Viola that Gargano and his crew were certifiable, and explained what they tried to do to me, I had to listen to him insist that I had lost my sense of humor. I informed the lieutenant that he and Gargano could both kiss my humorless ass. Furthermore I was going to stop over at the combat MPs' post and ask if the MPs could please eliminate the sniper before we lost one of Gargano's men and I would be blamed for killing the bastard.

Reporting to the MPs' post with my request for help, they said they would like to cooperate, but due to the condition of the church's steeple and lack of stairs, they being pretty well shot up, they could not help me. As I started to leave, the MP sergeant who had danced on the German tank mine raised his hand and said, "There are a few FFI (Free French of the Interior) in the area who would take the job for a pack of cigarettes." I agreed to the deal and the MP gave out a yell of, "Hey, Jacques, front and center."

I was surprised to see a young boy who looked about eleven years of age. He wore cut-off old army pants with rolled-up cuffs and a large ragged shirt with very deep pockets that held two concussion grenades tied to his belt. He carried a 46mm Mauser low on his hip, and it looked like the biggest damn murdering gun I had seen in the war. The kid also had crossed bandoliers onto which he had hooked clips for his Mauser. He looked as though he might weigh in at forty-two pounds fully clothed. His weapons weighed more than he did. He also had a pair of army paratrooper boots that were stuffed with papers and old rags, making him walk with an odd hop.

I originally thought he was a cripple. I questioned the MP about my taking the boy into the church, and the MP's answer was that Jacques was all man and could handle the job. "Right, Jacques?" and Jacques just nodded his head, "Yes." The kid had guts. When we bellied up to one of the large blown-out windows at the rear of the church, Jacques put his finger to his lips and signaled me to quietly follow him through the window, being careful that I did not step on the shards of glass on the floor. By this time I was feeling a little silly—a husky U.S. Army combat first sergeant following a little boy into a possible trap. As we circled toward the front of the church in search of a set of stairs that might lead up to the belfry, I watched as Jacques waved to me with the infantry signal for "quiet, enemy in sight." We both froze and Jacques indicated that there were more of the enemy in the upper area. They were eating their lunch, and not too quietly. He then removed his most precious possession—his paratrooper's boots— and indicated that I should remove mine and continue quietly after him.

I heard someone giggle and another person seemed to laugh in a snorting manner. I turned my head to watch Jacques. I could just see the bottoms of his very dirty feet, which I found out later were not dirty but bloody from the broken windows, disappearing over the sill and moving along the side of two broken rails nailed to the wall-ladder and into an upper room. A moment later Jacques' face peeked over the rim and his hand indicated that we had three people in the high point of the belfry and in the small area of the bell-room. They had climbed up using some wooden slats that had been nailed onto the wall to serve as a roughly built ladder. He also signaled for me to hurry down to the ground floor. But before I could move either up or down, I heard Jacques sliding quietly over his floor, which was my ceiling, toward the church's front. Then it became very quiet. Later Jacques told me that there were two men and one female there. They had been very friendly with the Germans, and they had been responsible for the deaths of quite a few of the French Underground by reporting their names to the Gestapo.

Jacques told me he had pulled the caps on the two potato grenades, then tossed both into the bell-room. After the explosion he had laid a sweep around the room with his BAR—a Browning automatic rifle and one hell of a deadly weapon. When I was able to climb up into the room for a look, Jacques had started to blow out the side of the church bell-room that faced Gargano's track and we could hear the crew's faint cheer of thanks. Jacques didn't pay much attention to the cheers. He was too busy making positive that all three people were dead.

Having never acquired the smoking habit, I gave the kid my battle jacket with its deep grenade pockets plus four packs of Lucky Strike cigarettes, enough barter material to make Jacques a wealthy young man.

This was not my last encounter with the FFI. They were very capable and very deadly. They had seen their parents and children killed, and they hated everything German, especially the SS and the bastardly Gestapo.

\* \* \*

Rumors. There were always rumors. But the one on the evening of July 16 turned out to be correct. We were going to make a major

LEROY E. DURKIN

move. Our First and Third Armies plus one British army would prepare to exit the Ste. Mere Eglise–St. Lo area following a major Allied air raid. It would involve 1,000 four-engine Lancasters and four-engine Halifaxes that would be coming over early the next morning. Fifteen hundred fortresses and liberators of the U.S. Eighth Air Force would be following them, along with 600 British and American medium bombers. It was the whole American Ninth Air Force and our entire tactical air force.

"They began forming them up back in England this morning," British Air Marshal Broadhurst is supposed to have said to General Bradley. "I don't really know what bit of air will be left unoccupied when the show starts." General Eisenhower corroborated that when he informed us that our attack was to be preceded "by what was the heaviest and most concentrated air assault hitherto employed in support of ground operations." Twelve thousand tons of bombs were to be dropped, 5,000 tons in less than forty-five minutes. A strong naval bombardment would be made to supplement the air effort.

On the sixteenth, we received the code word that alerted our half-tracks to exit our revetments combat prepared, then to travel through St. Lo following the directions of combat MPs that would be stationed along the way. When our code word, "squadron blue," came over our phones, we exited our revetments at approximately 10:40 hours. We could hear the roar of low-flying P-47 Thunderbolts with wing bombs and incendiaries crossing east to west in seven waves, two or three minutes apart.

The bombing planes were about forty degrees in the air from our ground positions, releasing their explosives a half-mile to a mile past our field positions. For more than an hour, 1,500 Flying Fortresses and Liberators dropped 3,341 tons of explosives. P-38 Lightnings followed in eight waves, each lasting about twenty minutes, laying more incendiaries. The 400 medium bombers, A-20s and B-26s, ran an attack on the southern end of the area with 500-pound bombs, concentrating on crossroads, especially German concentrations of tanks and troops.

During these six or seven hours of hell, the German antiaircrafts

64

were firing accurately and our planes were being hit. We could see them blowing up, burning on the way down. We saw parachutes on fire, holding twisting bodies kicking and clawing in the air. We saw crewmen falling with no chutes. One of our men murmured, "Dear God, those poor bastards are running as they are falling." A few men crossed themselves as one B-24 exploded in a huge ball of flames, spewing out its crew.

Finally, Sergeant Gargano yelled at me from his phone, "Sergeant, Captain says move the hell out, it's over." At least I think that's what he said. Due to three or four sudden, very close explosions that came right after the high bombers left, my ears were still ringing and my teeth were sore from clenching my jaws so tightly.

We later heard that, counting the different reloads and turnarounds, 2,000 planes participated in the bombing. As we moved through what had been the enemy's area the devastation was complete. Some of the enemy still tried to carry the war to us by firing on us. Most merely sat and stared blankly—at nothing. Their air force had never shown up.

We saw children playing amongst the bombed wrecks of buildings and the rubble that abounded at the sides of pockmarked roads. There were torn, hanging wires from telephone poles, uprooted trees, gutted horses and cows stinging your nose from the ghastly odors of the carnage. My mind kept saying over and over, *Why, why, dear God, why such a waste?*

Amidst the chaos a lone crew member of one of our planes was hanging with his chute caught in the cross braces of the only telephone pole still standing. The house next door had been split down the middle, exposing jagged slanting half walls with different soiled wallpapers and hanging pictures, parts of mattresses with destroyed beds—once someone's home, now a trashed dump with no walls. We hadn't personally destroyed houses like this, but it was sad to see nevertheless. One memory that stays in my mind was the sight of three little old men pushing a rickety three-wheel farmer's wagon slowly down a side street, searching for FFI members' sons and daughters who had been shot by the Germans two days earlier. Our passage line had been stopped and Sergeant Gargano's crew offered to share their dinner with the three men. When Gargano found out they could speak Italian he used one of our jeeps and shook down everybody along the stopped line, asking for smokes, old jackets, shoes, chocolate, extra K-rations, and GI blankets. I was very proud of Company D, but Lieutenant Viola was so happy he cried off and on for three days. Of course, Lieutenant Viola just happened to speak the language.

\* \* \*

I had been told many times that there must be one in every company. Felix Spizzica was ours—or should I say mine.

Felix was not stupid. He just never accepted being a soldier. His favorite line was "I am a civilian from Millville, New Jersey, I was abducted from my dad's barber shop; and if you bastards don't like it, send me home, first class!"

Felix would refuse to salute the captain, royally pissing him off. I personally chewed a chunk off of Felix's butt at least two or three times a day. When General Patton wandered into our area, he caught Felix thumbing his nose or shaking his jock. The general wasted the better part of a day chewing out our officers about the lack of military courtesy in their ranks

Small wonder that Felix remained a private through the entire war, even though he was awarded his Combat Infantry Badge and got a Bronze Arrow for participating in the invasions of France and six stars for different campaigns. But every time he made PFC, he would somehow screw up and lose his stripe.

Once Lieutenant Bill Green ordered Sergeant Gargano to have one of his men dig a straddle trench behind a clump of trees for the officers to use. Felix, being low man on the totem pole, got the job. A straddle trench is a trench two and a half feet deep, over which soldiers or officers straddle to relieve themselves, throwing a shovel full of dirt in afterward to deaden the stench.

I assigned the first noncom that entered my sight to accompany Felix and make sure that after digging the trench he policed the area and made a neat path to it. After giving them both complete instructions I informed them that when the trench was neatly completed they could have the balance of the day off to catch up with their V-mail. Then, having assigned the most important chore of the day, I started my rounds to the different gun crews to check their combat readiness.

Finding no problems at the first three crews, I started across the field toward my number four crew, whose revetment was about a hundred yards behind the place where I could see Felix and his keeper at work. I stopped for a moment or two and watched Felix through my field glasses. As I turned to walk over to the number four team and glanced across the field toward the area one more time, I witnessed one hell of a large fireball and explosion plus a lot of smoke.

I immediately yelled for Sergeant Rich to follow me to the explosion site with his medic and one other man. As we approached the area Felix was jumping up and down next to a very large hole that resembled a bomb crater, with smoke still curling upward from it. Felix's shirt was gone except for his sleeves, and so was his helmet. His keeper had obviously wet his pants. Neither one had been hurt. A crowd including our captain, executive officer, a farmer and his wife arrived at the same time. After ascertaining that no one had been injured, I beat the captain to it and asked Felix, "What the hell happened?"

Felix's answer was very simple to him. "I got sick and tired of trying to dig that f****** trench, especially when I kept hitting big stones and rocks, and that's when I had an idea. Why break my back trying to just dig the f****** trench? I borrowed three blocks of tri-nitro thyoline plus ten feet of primer cord. I put one block on each end and one in the middle of the hole that I had been able to dig. I attached the cord, set it off, and, holy cow—BANG, here's your trench!"

I looked at Felix, then at the captain and his executive officer. The farmer's wife was hysterical, sounding like a witch whose broom had just broken, screeching and shrieking in the farmer's ears. Finally the captain pointed at Felix, shook his head, and sent him to the medics for a checkup.

Our captain wore a patch over his left eye from an accidental backfire during basic training. I personally think he wore the patch to impress the Red Cross girls whenever they showed up with their coffee and skimmers. We always knew if Felix was in the vicinity because the Red Cross girls would be laughing at the faces he was making behind the captain's back and the nose thumbing he did on the captain's blind side. When the captain caught him doing that, Felix said he was "only picking my nose and the captain can't stop me from doing that."

\* \* \*

Felix managed to end up with considerably more than his share of dirty details throughout his enlistment. I turned Felix over to the tech sergeant in charge of communications, telling the sergeant to work the hell out of him. Finally, Felix could repair phone lines attached to the tops of telephone poles.

Whenever headquarters received information that one of our telephone lines had been severed due to an accident or by the enemy, someone had to follow the wire until the break was found and repaired. You always hoped that the enemy, who might be setting up an ambush for the lineman, didn't cause the break.

On a snowy, freezing November night near midnight a break was reported between Roye, France, and our headquarters and gun emplacements. As first sergeant I was alerted and contacted my tech sergeant. He contacted his staff sergeant, who aroused his buck sergeant, who called the corporal, who called a private first class, who passed it on to poor sad-sack Private Felix—the end of the line. He went out to check the line.

Our company was bunking that night in a bombed-out cellar. We had been warned that some SS paratroopers might be dropping in during the night, and to stay alert. I was checking out my army watch when the iron doors into the cellar were slammed open with a loud bang that sounded like a mortar round. Felix had returned.

Lieutenant Rother's bedroll was very close to the iron doors. The noise created a very pissed-off officer and most of the men were unable to go back to sleep. Lieutenant Rother loudly proclaimed, "Felix is solid bone upstairs, but he will do what you tell him to—bitching all the way." Of course Felix's vague salute to Rother was his F.D. wave, the personal salute that he practiced for the day when he became a civilian again. Then he would be able to tell all officers and first sergeants where to go and what to do.

Felix had an attitude. His favorite retort to me was "up yours," after I gave him a personal ass chewing for his attitude toward the U.S. Army. "Sergeant Durkin, for the amount of money the Army pays me a month, they are damned lucky I even associate with them, let alone salute you bastards. When we get home I'm going to tell everyone in town what an SOB you are." (He did!) That night, I looked at Felix and asked him for a report re the "wire break," i.e., how far out, how high off the ground, etc. His reply: "F.U."

Felix was a constant and totally spiteful pain in the butt to every officer and noncom who blundered into his path. But he was never confused; he was a civilian!

Incidentally, that was the night that Captain Glen Miller disappeared on his flight to Paris.

* * *

Somehow I was not surprised to learn that some shrewd sergeants had driven over to the airfield's headquarters and informed one of the staff sergeants that First Sergeant Durkin would like to borrow one of their extra pot-bellied stoves to help ward off the chilling and damp wind that leaked under his tent. A damned lie if I ever heard one. They wanted the stove for *their* tent, where they had set up their big gambling casino.

Once the stove was operational some of the cold and damp dissipated. The men threw anything into the stove that would burn—old socks, underwear, damp wood, whatever would keep the potbelly red-hot and glowing. I guessed the games had been in session for about four or five hours when one of the cooks opened the tent flaps and yelled, "For the second call, chow's on. Come and get it." Nobody moved. The losers continued to piss and moan and the winners kept on playing and counting their gains.

About twenty minutes later a tent flap was quietly lifted and pulled aside by a six-foot-one-inch, very annoyed staff sergeant named Jimmy Adams. He was a no-nonsense headquarters mess sergeant, a very tough soldier from the hills of Tennessee. Aside from a couple of onlookers who greeted Jim, no one paid much attention when he approached the hot and glowing stove. Quietly lifting the lid with its handle, Jim removed the stove's red-hot lid and dropped a full clip of ammunition onto the red-hot coals. He quickly replaced the lid, and blowing his whistle, yelled, "When I call time for chow, damn it, I mean NOW, not when you bastards feel like it."

Walking out the door and turning his head, Jim gestured toward the stove, blew his whistle one more time and yelled, "I dropped a full clip of .30 caliber ammunition into your stove," just as the first few rounds exploded, blowing the lid off the stove. There was a mass exodus through the opened tent flap, but the combined weight of the mob plus pieces of red-hot stove shrapnel ripped out one complete side of the tent. There were guys tripping over chair legs, arms and asses tumbling—trying to get out of the gaming area. Utter chaos!

After his prank, Jim felt as though number 7 tent deserved some kind of apology from him for blowing up their priceless stove and setting the north side of their tent on fire. Maybe the real reason for the apology was that he got wind of a stupid plan being made by a couple of angry sergeants from tent 7. They were talking about setting off a piece of primer cord—TNT—under Sergeant Adams' footlocker while he was sleeping. Of course the stupid, jackass sergeants did not consider the high probability that any exploding primer cord under the footlocker would be the end of Jimmy and a few tent mates. Anyway, Sergeant Adams was most humble during the understandably wild lineup for chow, having told his cooks to serve doubles and triples to everyone that could handle it, especially to double and triple-up on the peach and apple pies.

The following day, taking the threats against his life seriously,

Adams ordered his cooks to inform everyone that about "two clicks" (two miles) up the road there was a café-roadhouse that sported a hot French band and featured a world-renowned chanteuse and a backup chorus line of gorgeous young dancing ladies. Sergeant Adams had already cleared with our captain the booking of the café for the evening. All personnel were welcome, including the officers who helped in the confiscation of a truck from their officer friends at the airfield. We needed the truck to transport a load of wine from the partially bombed-out local wine factory that we had just liberated. Talk about good and bad luck running together.

We had tried to take an inventory in the huge pile of rubble that had once been a factory, but the main result of that was to create in short order a bunch of drunks who had once been soldiers. Fortunately, there were a few honest men taking the inventory because we found a few intact bottles of champagne, cognac, Calvados and pink champagne. These were to be delivered to the cafe's back door as a special treat. Festivities at the bar would open at 19:30 hours and the stage show would start promptly at 20:00 hours. We were going to have some party!

* * *

The real reason for Sergeant Adams' apology was not that he felt remorse. He just did not feel comfortable around those very nutty soldiers. He knew they had access to TNT, primer cords, grenades, and all kinds of weapons. A couple of noncoms from tent 7, while trying to escape from the tent, said they had nearly broken an arm and an ankle. Supply Sergeant Digger claimed his nose was nearly broken. He had received a black eye, which he swore was the result of a pair of hits by a guy from the motor pool but he wasn't sure that Sergeants Gargano and Smith weren't the culprits.

There were even a few rumors that a couple of poor losers from the crap game were complaining loudly and also hatching plans to sneak a couple of strings of primer cords under Adams' cot while he was asleep. We had quite a few Tennessee noncoms and soldiers in

71

our outfit, and some of them wanted some form of sweet revenge. Sergeant Adams was constantly saying that he was from the "hills of wonderful Tennessee" and he knew that his ass was in deep trouble with the Tennessee boys. A lot of them were saying, to hell with shooting the SOB, it will be more fun to get on with his lynching.

With tears running down his cheeks (probably from holding in his laughter) Sergeant Adams said he would never do such a thing again. Although his cooks seemed very subdued during the next chow lineup, a couple of them baked extra tasty peanut butter cookies and prepared some mouth-watering submarine sandwiches for later consumption at the party.

At 7:45 the motor pool delivered to the back flap of the cooking tent two truckloads of raucous, happy soldiers. Some of the men were legally too young to drink stateside but nobody cared. They were already half-smashed and yelling for that beautiful chanteuse and her backup beautiful, sweet, young dancing ladies.

That afternoon, I thanked the good Lord, modified orders had just been handed to me. After three weeks on point we had been removed from combat status and ordered to check and repair all weapons. Also we were given a forty-eight-hour grace period in which we were to turn in shot-up, broken, worn or torn equipment. We would each receive three pairs of new socks and shorts, plus a new jacket, pants, and shirts. We also were to be allowed ten minutes under a portable shower. This was our first change of clothes and our first shower in two and a half weeks.

Our forty-eight-hour repair time would go very fast, but it didn't take long before most of the new tents we moved into were supporting some type of poker or crap game. The guys involved folded their cots and moved them into one corner of their pyramidal tents. In one tent, a large tool chest had been borrowed from the motor pool and laid on its side, making a half-assed table for the gamblers.

The jokes were flying. Everyone was smiling. Since we had landed in France, we had dipped our uniforms into a drum of gasoline once in a while, hoping to kill not only our odor but our unfriendly bug visitors—the scabies, lice and other creatures looking for a new home away from the bombed-out houses, barns, and chicken coops we frequented when we went looking for eggs and other edibles.

A couple of my buck sergeants had taken a truck down to the wine factory for a few cases of grape and Calvados. Just smelling the wine factory had them humming! I had the second platoon's guards secure all weapons for the duration of the party.

At 8 p.m. festivities were underway, at least with the drinks, cookies and sandwiches. But most of the men and the under-age drunks were yelling and stamping on the floor, waiting to see the "lovely chanteuse" and the young dancing ladies. Then, with the loud roll of the drums, the bandleader stepped out, holding a pink kazoo over his head and trying to lead and play his kazoo at the same time. This may have scared the band, which wasn't ready to play. Their opening was a complete disaster.

The leader was trying to get the drummer's attention by throwing his wand at him. Instead he accidentally hit a senorita who kicked out and stumbled onto the stage, followed by the dancing girls. Everyone was expecting a beautiful young senorita dream girl with a lovely voice. Hers was the opposite. She had a shrill voice that cut to the bone. The senorita motioned and out slipped the girls of the chorus, minus shoes, attempting to back up the senorita. Unfortunately, four were tone deaf and the fifth was an obvious transvestite who did not know the song.

The room roared in various stages of drunken hysteria. A couple of men started to mock the senorita by singing "I Surrender, Dear." She was dressed in some kind of costume that was supposed to make her look like an American Indian squaw. Actually, her bare midriff exposed her navel, which was adorned with a wine cork. She wore imitation diamond rings on her fingers and some poor MP's left armband on one of her hairy arms. She had acquired an old Mickey Mouse watch somewhere, and it was dangling from the other arm as an ornament.

Felix was throwing kisses to her as he climbed on a chair and up on the stage, trying to lead her tenderly into a dance step. Then he fell flat on the stage, passing gas with all the force of a pregnant cow. That seemed to disturb the bandleader. He and the drummer began arguing with Felix, who was now loudly insisting the band stay in tune with la senorita. By then, the band leader was giving Italian salutes to the total house. This challenged Felix to attempt to get the total gang to sing along with him:

*"There's a burlesque theatre where the guys love to go, to see Queenie, the cutie of the burlesque show. Take it off, take if off, cry the boys from the rear. Take it off, take it off, soon it's all you can hear But she's always a lady even in pantomime. She stops and always just in time!"*

The poor senorita was doing her best. The girls had done their best. It just wasn't enough for this drunken crowd. As the senorita moved to center stage and tried to curtsy, she lost her balance and with a loud screech she and her trinkets made one hell of a crash as she fell into the drums in the pit. The sleeping drunks awoke with the feeling that they were under a mortar barrage. The assemblage rose, cast ceremony to the winds, and rushed for the doors like a mob, overturning chairs, tables smashing crockery, bottles, tugging, struggling, shouldering, crowding. It seemed they would do anything to escape the senorita, who was now making demon-like threats to hang the frigging leader of the band.

I ordered the leader of the band to try to calm the men by playing one more song, "Coming 'Round the Mountain." But she was right. They were terrible. I gave her permission to hang the whole band. This served only to goad her on, her silver bell of a tongue making the flesh crawl. Then she started to tear at her orange-red hair with her green fingernails. Next she screeched, bowed, and gave Felix the finger. Finally, she turned around and mooned the bandleader, then spun around once and mooned what was left of the audience before tripping off the stage—carrying one of our full bottles of Calvados.

What a madhouse! Everyone was near drunk, partly drunk or totally drunk. As we left, Adams grabbed my arm and groaned that the wine must have been tainted, because some of his cooks had kicked open the cafe's partially destroyed door and were now sleeping in a big pile of snow, sounding like a bunch of happy, grunting, snug, comfortable hawgs. As soon as the cold air hit Adams, he started to try to speak to me again but was only able to utter, "I mush be ordly can't voomit." These were his last words before he tripped and fell right on top of one of his drunken Tennessee buddies.

None of us was prepared for the deep accumulation of snow. It had been just a dusting before we had gone to the café. It took at least three quarters of an hour to load the two trucks with the drunks. The cold air had some of them sober and walking by the time we reached our area. I ordered extra sleeping time for all, one extra blessing to be tacked on to the end of our never-to-be-forgotten "it's great to be alive" party.

* * *

I had asked Sergeant Joe Smith, who loved to drive a jeep whenever one was available, to wait with me at the café to make sure that all men and equipment had been accounted for. So we were the last ones to leave. The snow had stopped. The sky was very clear, but the wind and the jeep were brutally cold. Joe took a shortcut across a field, and we had some trouble maneuvering out of a slight snow bank. We were both involved in that when Joe noticed a uniformed man standing in the quite-bright moonlight. Due to the moon's reflection in the fresh snow, the man's ragged uniform was very clear. It wasn't one of ours. He was a German from a tiger tank company, a definite enemy. In the moonlight it was easy to see that his legs were encased in a pair of muddy German officer's boots and the knees of his britches were torn. He had a dirty old rag wrapped around his left knee.

He was not a man who seemed young, and I guessed he was about my age—a very old twenty-two or twenty-three. Standing alongside Joe, I realized that all three of us were battle worn and exhausted. I looked at the face of my enemy, a German noncom, as luck would have it an "oberst feld webel," as he tendered his side arm, a long-barreled Magnum .46 caliber pistol. He extended it butt first, a gesture of "I give up." Sergeant Joe started to move, but I cautioned him as I continued looking into the dull tired eyes of a man who had had enough. It was so absurd to be standing with an enemy when a couple of days ago we had tried so hard to kill each other. To this day, and it will always be so, I can't remember ever being more perplexed. I said, "Vie gates," to him and Joe gave him a cigarette, holding a trembling match for him.

Who were we? Why were we standing here? I turned to Joe, who gestured towards a medic's jeep that had just arrived, and had been searching for us. I advised the second jeep about our prisoner and they requested that we follow them back to camp. I also informed them that the prisoner spoke excellent English and had surrendered his weapons. Because of the cold I borrowed an army blanket from the medics and wrapped it around the prisoner's shoulders. Before he moved over to the medic's jeep, a man of exquisite dignity, the oberst clicked his heels and bowed to both Joe and me, offering each of us his hand. He watched my eyes and observed my reaction. I shook his hand, Joe shrugged his shoulder and smiled at me as the jeep left, with a prisoner whose dignity seemed to state, "I'm not beaten. I've simply had enough." I still have his .46 caliber long-barreled Magnum pistol.

\* \* \*

Due to the elimination of a large portion of German air power by the British and American air forces, our antiaircraft company was split up and reassigned as infantry support. My company was assigned to the Third Army. Consequently we drew food rations, underwear, socks and everything else from any place that we could scrounge them.

The orders from General Patton's Army Headquarters were to use a couple of our platoon's half-tracks as points. The tracks were to proceed down identified roads until fired upon by the enemy, at which time the tracks were to eliminate the enemy, if possible. If enemy forces were too strong, tracks were to request air or other support.

After two-plus weeks of this type of a split-up war, a run of uncooked chow, cold coffee, and no water for washing, a General Patton aide issued a new order. Combat soldiers would be issued one canteen of water per day and every soldier would save enough water from his canteen to shave each day. The general said, "A shaved soldier will maintain a source of pride in himself and his unit."

There was also a shortage of toilet paper and Third Army combat soldiers would each be allowed only eight sheets a day. We were not to gripe about the screwup, however. In General Patton's words, we were to use a "handful of the deciduous growths of a plant, which may be substituted for toilet paper." In other words, we were to use dry tree leaves as a substitute for our civilian toilet tissue.

Eight sheets a day may not sound so bad, but there is an old adage that bad things come in pairs or threes. Most of us were not only sore as hell, but also as sure as hell up to our limits with the pairs concept. We ran out of potable drinking water, and most of us had by that point also run out of water tablets. In the field it's an absolute necessity to have drinking water. But without water tablets to render the water we found drinkable, we were likely to get diarrhea. We were very sad sacks, one hell of a sad sight to see.

We called diarrhea the "big D" or the "GI trots," because men were leaving their positions and trotting off in all directions, usually at least once every two or three hours. Because most latrines were occupied, slit trenches were filled to near overflow. Not a major problem, you think? I forgot to mention the cramps and heaves, plus all of the guys who didn't make it to a latrine or a slit trench.

It seems remarkable that no one laughed, although, if you think it over, no one would laugh at a dozen men with diarrhea and the heaves, especially if those men were armed, using loaded rifles as canes under a very hot French sun with damned little relief in sight. If the enemy had only known. Different gun crews could not see the sense in posting security guards. Most of the men were wishing that someone would kill them, putting them out of their extreme, despicable, wretchedness. Most guns crews thought they should be awarded some type of a substitute for the Purple Heart and call it the "Bleeding Butt."

Because of severe cramps, vomiting, dehydration, and the continual problem of trying to clean our drawers in our tin helmets, always in between our trips to the woods or behind the hedgerows, like a bunch of dogs, everyone of us was miserable. If you had diarrhea it was pure hell. If you somehow didn't have it, you had to deal with buddies who reeked with the smell of human waste for days on end under a very hot sun.

The time was 1400 and I had just returned from filling in my third hole of the day when I was ordered to attend our division's supply officer at battalion headquarters. The supply officer was normally a very cheerful and capable first lieutenant. Today, with "the big D," he walked like a severe cripple, aggravated by his inability to obtain medical assistance. Nearing the end of our fourth big D-day, with a reported sixty-eight soldiers whose combat effectiveness was decreasing by the hour and the knowledge that that number would probably double by the next day, the lieutenant was not a happy camper.

Instead of returning my salute, he asked me if I couldn't clean myself up a little better, because we had been ordered to meet with our division's general. I gave the lieutenant the old Durkin evil eye and the lieutenant yelled, "Yes, damn it. Both of us are to report, and you stink!"

The general's office was in the town's partially destroyed mayor's office. The first thing I noticed as we entered was a converted bedroom with a wide-open door into an adjoining bathroom, with one of its walls blown out. The second thing I saw was a very fat cushion that the general was sitting on. After a brief moment or two of a pissed-off stare, the general took a very deep breath and began to explain why he personally was pissed off and how damned sore his gut and ass were. Plus he was GD tired of having his conversations interrupted because some goddamned rude SOB wanted to tell me how sore his butt was. Plus he had to cut the phone calls short because he had to take his eighth crap of the day and it was only noon.

"Lieutenant," the general said, his voice rising, "do you know that at least two thirds of this division's soldiers are out there crapping their brains out all over the whole damned countryside? Also, Lieutenant, can you tell me why my men are being subjected to the same type of GI trots that Washington's and Napoleon's men experienced?" As the general turned his head and looked at me, I thought, *Oh, shit. It's my turn in the barrel.* Instead, the general asked me with a sigh, "Well, Top Sergeant, how in the hell is your ass?"

Turning back to the lieutenant the general grunted, "I want you two to find a way to get this division some water tablets. Now. And I mean right now. Last but not least, I want some extra toilet paper in this division, and I don't give a rat's ass how you get it. Damn it, Lieutenant, move your ass before something jumps up and bites us on our very sore asses!"

The General shifted his butt on his cushion, looked at us both and said, "Lieutenant, unless you have an extra problem you are dismissed."

The lieutenant answered with a very sharp salute, and a "Sir, I need to use your john."

The general looked at me and asked, "First Sergeant, how about you?"

I looked the general right in the eyes, and thought to myself, *Durkin, this is the closest you will ever get to a general.* And with true feeling, I saluted and said, "Sir, can I use your crapper? I gotta go bad."

The general's reaction: "Be my guest, Top!"

Soon after I left the general's crapper I hustled to a little stream for a quick bath, unaware of the habits of the up-creek users—the farmer's horses, pigs, cows, three bulls, goats, etc. that had been relieving themselves in it. I told Sergeant Smith, who was bathing along with me, that he and the water smelled like a chemical lavatory gone wrong. Me too!

Most soldiers in France could sing these words to the tune of "Here Comes the Bride":

*Eight sheets a day Eight sheets a day*
*With no water tablets It's sure hell to pay!*

\* \* \*

With my naked eye I could see the HE-111 airplanes sailing out from the white clouds and moving slowly across the sky, followed by a series of black puffs. At their estimated distance the bombs' impacts sounded more like a few muffled thumps and an occasional rolling thunderstorm. Snatching my German-freed binoculars from our track and putting them to my eyes, I saw the bombers come considerably closer. They were big, twin-engine planes, painted with crosses and swastikas. The HE-111s seemed very long when compared with the ME-109s and as seen through the glasses they had a scary appearance, like flying freight boxcars.

Of course Sergeant Smith said, "They're not heading this way. They seem to be heading away." As usual, Smitty was wrong. The thumps became louder and Smitty said, "It's sort of like a summer storm rolling toward you." A distant whistling noise became more loud and shrill, followed by a sudden ear clap, as though you had been given a resounding slap to your head and ear. Three or four sudden, very close explosions came, one right on top of the others.

Sergeant Smith looked up and yelled, "Let's get the hell out of here." At least that's what I thought he said; my ears were still ringing.

I told him, "Stay loose. I think the thumps seem to be moving away, but we have to beware of any strafing fighters." As if to directly contradict me, the thumps suddenly seemed to be coming closer. Thump, thump, thump, thump, THUMP.

I was point and Sergeant Smith was covering my rear with a BAR, alert for any sudden move from one of the wrecks we were passing that used to be called homes. There was rubble everywhere and odors of dead people and animals. High up on a telephone pole we passed, a paratrooper with his chute half-opened still hung. He had probably been there since the first days of the invasion.

We were too busy and too stupid to be scared. I turned around suddenly in time to see Smitty wave for three men of Dog platoon to move up closer to me, along with four men from Able platoon. The fact that two of them were medics gave me a hell of a good feeling, almost of security. I horse-whispered to Smitty, "Don't forget to let me know when we are having fun." Moving up to a corner house, I peered around the corner and looked down the street. It was empty of anything alive except for two men loading dead people into a two-wheeled cart. A few bodies still lay on the cobblestones.

One man, covered with blood, was picking the cadavers up one at a time by their arms and thrusting them at the other man, who was trying to stack them in the cart. I felt Smitty coming up beside me and I heard Joe gasp at what he saw. The two men had picked up the nearly nude body of an old scrawny woman whose gray pubic hair showed through the pink rag still hanging on her.

Smitty picked up a large stone and motioned that I should rap the stock of my carbine to get the attention of the men loading the cart. I motioned for them to take time out for a brief talk as they moved over to us. They were tired and filthy, their odor beyond description. I pointed up to where the body of the paratrooper was still hanging and asked if they could get him down. They said that two of them had been killed by snipers while trying to lower the trooper, but said they would try again after agreeing that it was no way for a hero to be treated. We gave them each a pack of cigarettes and two packs of C rations, and thanked God we did not have their job. By the way, they called themselves "The Death Platoon."

\* \* \*

As the remnants of our platoon spread out I sent Sergeant Smith and his men back down an alley to make sure no one was following us, hoping to set us up for an ambush. The rest of us continued slowly through the village toward the manor house at the top of a slight rise. As we began our ascent it became obvious that the manor house was a very large estate with a couple of large barns and a large, four-hole outhouse. One hell of a firefight had raged in the vicinity of the barns, which now housed swollen dead horses stinking in their paddocks. Clouds of fat black flies surrounded the barns and occasionally settled stickily on our faces and hands.

Whoever had shot up the farm had been very thorough. There were dead cats, a couple of dead dogs, and a lot of dead rats near each dead animal. As Joe moved cautiously around to the front side of one barn I heard vomiting and some screeching cuss words. I followed him and saw Smitty crying, cussing and sick, standing in the middle of the prone bodies of five small children who had been machine-gunned. How could this happen? The killing of children, turning living people into stiff, glassy-eyed dead garbage, torn into pieces and abandoned amongst dead rats, cats and chickens—this was not war, it was slaughter.

As we stood there in our grief and anger, without surprise or fear we saw at the same instant three thick Vs of German planes coming out of the northeast. The first wave was ME-109s in a strafing formation, spitting out black smoke. We heard the unmistakable sound of their 20mm guns tearing down the street toward our position, leaving small and large holes in the cement road and tearing chunks from what little was left of the front of the city hall at our end of the street. As they flew away, I wondered if my eyes resembled Joe's, which had a demonic and crazed look. But we continued our job. The Germans had pulled back and we were in control of Roye, actually a small village wrapped around a train station.

"I'll be damned," I said and looked at Joe's helmet with amazement. He had a perfect hole in it that had entered the left side and exited the right side—a perfect "pinky hole." He said he hadn't felt a damn thing—nothing. What dumb luck! I shook my head and growled, "Joe, the good Lord must have an entire group of angels assigned just to keep your dumb ass out of trouble."

Joe's standard retort followed, "Screw you, Durkin." Then he said, "I need, oh, shit, help me find a new helmet or a high hat." That was laughable because Sergeant Smith was always checking out different closets and cellars for different kinds of goodies, taking very stupid risks and completely disregarding the possibility of booby traps. Joe was especially good in a cellar where the wine and plums were stored.

I remember one time Joe found a closet that had a really weird man's plaid suit with three-inch cuffs in it. He thought the suit fit him, and he found a top hat in the closet to go along with it. I remember Lieutenant Purdie looking him over, choking as he laughed and said, "You really want to know how you look? I'll tell you how you look. In that suit and hat you look like a G.D. California clap doctor." I personally had never seen a Californian clap doctor, but Joe told Lieutenant Purdie that he should go screw himself, because when he looked into a broken looking glass, he though he looked cool.

Lieutenant Purdie looked at me, looked at Joe in his suit, and told me to start counting to twenty-five. If Joe hadn't changed back to his army clothes and set that masquerade piece of crap on fire he was going to order me to kick the crazy bastard in his balls. Joe then had the nerve to ask Purdie if he could put the clothes and hat in his duffle bag, promising not to wear them until he got home or he could he send them to his dad to save for him. Lieutenant Purdie looked at me, shook his head, gave Joe a stare and said, "OK, but only if you promise to wear that plaid suit and top hat to our first reunion in New York."

\* \* \*

September 1944 was one miserable month. Cold persistent rain caused debilitating problems among the troops. Then there was a blanket order from General Patton's Third Army to all combat forces for immediate implementation. "Due to a deficiency of brass in the States, all combat troops were to police each and every brass cartridge regardless of size without fail, after every engagement and prior to vacating the area."

This was received without enthusiasm. Sergeant Joe and I discussed the complications of the order. Each of our half-tracks could expend 3,500 fifty-caliber rounds per minute. That would create a monumental cleanup task under peacetime conditions, let alone when we were being strafed or under a firefight condition.

Soon after the order was handed down, Sergeant Joe was about to go out on point, but first he assigned two of his crew, Private Alexis and PFC Wilson, to be responsible for the transport of brass to battalion headquarters. Giving me a mock salute and with a wave of his hand, Sergeant Smith drove off, standing up on the passenger side of his track and blowing his claxon horn in a wise-ass attempt to mimic General Patton. Whenever possible, General Patton loved to hitch a ride standing up on the passenger side of a half-track, saluting all troops on both sides of the road.

I finished my rounds, checking on everyone's combat readiness, ammunition, fuel, etc. and returned to headquarters. About an hour and a half later I received a radio message to the effect that Sergeant Smith was still on point, and he had not answered his last two check-in calls. This was very rare for Smith, and my first thought was that he might possibly have been ambushed. I borrowed the captain's jeep with its mounted .50 caliber machine gun and corporal driver. I took along my confiscated BAR.

We took off down the same road Joe had taken. With crossed fingers, I estimated that Smith had penetrated about eight to ten kilometers into enemy territory. With our machine gun manned, and all of our senses fully alerted, we were expecting some type of ambush. We found Sergeant Smith's half-track parked about fourteen kilometers farther into enemy territory and still on point. I did a double take when I saw a one-star general's command car parked about fifteen feet behind the half-track.

Sergeant Smith and his crew were standing at a very relaxed attention facing a muddied, helmetless, very wrinkled, and extremely pissed-off brigadier general. This was one of our truly "Don't tread on me" leaders. He was violently and systematically screaming at Smith and his crew.

As our jeep slid on the muddy and slippery ground I jumped out. As soon as I could, without breaking my GI butt, I gave the general a sad-sack, half-assed salute and came to a lousy approximation of attention. I was then informed by the general in a loud falsetto that he had removed Sergeant Smith's stripes for insubordination plus an attitude unbecoming a U.S. Army noncom. He had also broken Smith's second-in-command and gunner, Corporal James. James already held a Purple Heart and a Bronze Star for honorable action above and beyond the line of duty, but the general said he was breaking him because he had been disrespectful. It seems he had laughingly called the general "His Honor."

The general went on to say that if he had the time he would look up our colonel and captain and explain to them what military courtesy meant. Then he started to hiccup and belch, screaming at the top of his voice, "If this were World War I, I would have you and your captain up on charges. G.D. it, do you understand me, you and your frigging crew? Believe you me, this is not the last you will hear about this screwed-up action. I am a general, G.D. it! My poor half-assed jeep driver is more of a soldier than any of this crew."

The general's face was very red, and as he turned around, I clicked the heels of my combat boots together and damned near put out my right eye by saluting him. The SOB didn't even try to return my high ball. He gave Sergeant Smith and his crew one last crackerjack of a pissed-off look as he left the scene, pointing in the wrong direction, and yelling at his poor PFC driver, "You stupid idiot, you were going in the wrong direction." As they drove on, we could hear him shouting. Why in the hell was he, the general, so unlucky as to wind up with all of the f****** screw-ups in this f****** army of misfits and half-assed sergeants?

Seeing that his direction was incorrect, I tried to flag down the general's driver. As they turned they damned near ran over me. I think they meant to hit both Smith and me.

As soon as the general was out of sight, I asked Sergeant Smith, "What the hell was that all about, and why did you miss your call-ins?"

He started to grin as he told me what had happened. "Being point and following orders to the best of our ability, we were looking for, and destroying, any of the enemy that fired on us with intent to harm us. In other words, we were doing our job. We were going in harm's way, hell bent on wiping out a dangerous and able bunch of Nazi bastards, before they could terminate our track and crew.

"Sergeant Durkin," he continued, "I followed your orders perfectly and assumed Company D's point for the Third Army, following to the letter your orders to find and destroy any and all of the enemy that fired on us with intent to kill us."

I looked at Joe suspiciously and said, "OK, give me your side of the story."

"This road leads to a village and a small town," he said, "both held by SS troops with automatic weapons. We had skirted the village and were coming up on the backside of the town when we were fired on by two or three machine guns from the second floor of a large brick building. We were expecting that and were ready for the machine guns. There were also a 20mm anti-tank cannon and some snipers in the right corner ground floor. Although their fire was erratic, it was dangerous. Consequently, we pulled into a defilade for cover and opened up on the second floor of the building with our quads" (four .50 caliber machine guns that can deliver 3,500 rounds per minute automatically) "and proceeded to blow the hell out of the German machine gun nests. We also sprayed the ground floor and shut down their 20mm."

Sergeant Smith took a short breath and continued, "I became aware that a vehicle had pulled up behind us and that some loudmouth SOB was screaming 'Cease fire, damn it! Cease fire right now, all of you! Who in the hell is in charge. G.D. it, can't you hear me? I am a general, damn it to hell. Don't you frigging idiots understand that I am ordering all of you to shut down that G.D. weapon at once? You are using too much f****** ammunition and wasting the taxpayers' money.'

"So, I stopped the action, saluted the general, who didn't return my salute, but started to yell at everybody in my crew, 'Police the brass, pick up every damned brass cartridge, now! You will remove your helmets and start picking up brass and put them in your helmets.' Sergeant Durkin, only an idiot would order the removal of helmets in a combat area, regardless of a priority. The general's face looked as though he was having a case of apoplexy or a heart attack, and he kept screaming about the frigging taxpayers' money, and then he started choking and coughing and screaming, 'Pay attention, every G.D. one of you.'

"Sergeant Durkin, I kept trying to do everything the general ordered us to do, but so help me God, if I ever hear anybody tell me to pick up the brass again, I'm going to make them another bung hole. About this time the general said something nasty about our mothers, and Felix mumbled, 'Go screw yourself, General,' just loud enough for the general to hear him. And the general got very red in his face and he started yelling, 'Which sad sack of crap said that? I'm a general and I want respect, and I want all of this brass picked up.' Then he tried to pick up some brass and his feet slipped in the mud, only making him angrier. Then he told his driver to start looking for either a sharp knife or a bayonet so his driver could remove my stripes. Actually, I though the SOB was going to try and cut my throat. He was really weird.

"He took Felix's PFC stripe and said Felix was the dumbest SOB he ever met from Brooklyn. Felix told him 'General I ain't never been in Brooklyn or any other f****** town in Florida.' This really set the general off again. He called us a mob of numb nuts and peckerheads, G.D. tenderfoot Boy Scouts playing at war and just wasting the taxpayers' money by shooting up that poor old brick building. He just kept chewing out all of our asses. And right then, because he had stopped our firing, the Germans got back into action and opened up with one of their machine guns. They hit our track and the general's vehicle with pretty damned accurate firing. Some real live rounds came very close to the general, making the general dive under our half-track on his belly and in the mud.

"Then he started to really yell at me," Smith said. "'Sergeant, return fire, G.D. it! Open up! Are you hard of hearing? Can't you hear me? Damn it, Sergeant, open fire at once, right this minute. I'm a general and I'm in danger because of your stupidity. Sergeant, I'm ordering you to shoot those Nazi bastards at once.'

"That's when Felix leaned over the side of the track and emptied two helmets full of brass, making a hell of a racket," Joe said. "I was very polite, and I told him, 'Your Honor, I'm not a sergeant anymore because the general broke all of the noncoms, and besides, General, we all agree with you about wasting the taxpayers' money.' And honestly, Sergeant Durkin, the general yelled at me, 'Don't argue with me. Screw the taxpayers and their frigging civilian money. Just kill those Nazi bastards before they kill me. Sergeant, don't you understand me?'

"So, we followed the general's orders, but first I leaned over and yelled to the general, 'Sir, are you sure you want us to commence firing?' and he yelled, 'Yes, damn it. To hell with the taxpayers. Screw 'em. They're just a bunch of rich, damn civilians.' Sergeant Durkin, we opened up with everything we had. Taxpayers' money be damned."

Joe said, "Felix was very conscientious and very polite, and he kept leaning over the iron back of our track and asking the general, 'Sir, do you still want us to pick up the brass?' Sergeant Durkin, I swear, every time I leaned under the tracks to tell the general, 'Sir, do you still want us to keep firing?' he would choke up or hiccup and belch. But he always answered, 'Yes, G.D. it, yes!'

"Look at the building. As you can see, Sergeant Durkin, we pulverized the Germans' position. The whole back of the building was destroyed and I informed the general that we had eliminated the Germans' guns and His Honor didn't even say, 'Good work.' He just belched, hiccupped and then, honest, Sergeant, he may have soiled his pants. He let go a very loud burp from the wrong end. We all heard it. Then he started to crawl out from under the tracks on his hands and knees and I started to brush off the mud from his blouse and pants. I accidentally brushed off one of his stars that had come loose. When he was finally able to stand up, he tripped into me and I stepped on his star. When I said, 'Oh, shit,' the general said, 'What the hell is wrong?' I told him, 'I think I stepped on one of your stars.' About this time Felix interrupted and asked the general if he could maybe get a medal for helping to save His Honor's ass, because he would like to write home and tell his pop.

"And that's about when you came on the scene, Sergeant Durkin. By the way, can we get our stripes back?"

I said, "Hell, yes. You guys never lost them. Get back on point and report your total action—the KO of the Nazis' machine guns and cannon, and especially make sure you tell the captain which direction you think the general was going the last time you saw his command car. At least cover your ass!"

Sergeant Smith made his report via his radio to our captain, who told our colonel about the action and the general's participation. They laughed so hard they nearly cried. They confirmed that Sergeant Smith was truly following orders, which were to proceed northeast until he was fired upon, then to return fire. When I wrote up my report of the incident to Battalion, I recommended that Sergeant Joe Smith be awarded a fourth stripe, to become a staff sergeant, ASAP. And that's what happened.

* * *

When two or three soldiers started out as protectors of each other at the beginning of a combat situation, they usually stayed together. There were practical reasons for that. One is how we fixed up the bottom of a trench so that we could sleep in it. We used one of our raincoats, spread out over the very bottom. Next we put one of our overcoats over the raincoat. Next came both blankets. We put the other overcoat on top of the blankets and finally put the second raincoat on top, to keep the dampness off our sleeping pile.

However, every once in a while the movement of troops in a company make it necessary to change foxholes. That's how the following tale just happened to happen.

We had just taken over guard duty of a very large dam that held back a fresh and clear, large lake. If the enemy were to blow up that dam, a village and an apple orchard near the dam would be wiped out, creating a vast roadblock and knocking out a few crossroads, one of which was a highway into Paris.

In good weather we usually hit the sack at the same time. I chose someone to be sergeant of the guard, who along with any posted guards would stay up until he first woke the cooks up at 4:30 and then woke me up.

After chow one night, before hitting the sack, Sergeant John Povaznik, our head cook, brought two of his cooks over to where we

89

had started to dig our trench. He told me that, as punishment, they were going to dig a damned good sleeping trench for he and I to share. "And it better be perfect," he said as he turned two shovels over to the cooks. Meanwhile, he and I were going to take a swim in the lake.

When we arrived at the lake behind the dam, we handed our sergeant of the guard a box of fresh doughnuts, and I relieved him while he delivered doughnuts to his men. John went to the water's edge, stripped down and began washing his clothes, wringing them out and hanging them in the branches of nearby apple trees to dry. I did the same.

Sergeant John was one hell of a good soldier as well as a top cook. But when he lost he temper or got excited, his Polish heritage often took over, and no one understood what the hell he was saying. As luck would have it, in a clearing not far from John's bare-ass swim, there happened to be a little old Gypsy washing her clothes from the rear of her home caravan with her mule grazing nearby; John spotted her, saw me buck naked and began yelling at me in Polish. The Gypsy, hearing a familiar language, started toward John, speaking Polish to him. I assumed it was Polish because I sure as hell was at a loss to understand her.

After a lengthy conversation, John turned to me and said, "Let her tell your fortune, Top, for a candy bar, or a couple of cigs. I'll translate for you."

Reluctantly, but now clothed, having pulled on my pants, I agreed. It's funny, after all these years, how clearly I recall the intensity on the little old lady's face when she looked up from my outstretched hand and announced, in shattered English, "Your fortune is good." And then she pointed to my lifeline, running her finger slowly up my hand, saying, "You will live a very good healthy life. You will be fairly wealthy…" Then she stopped, made a "tishtish" sound with her tongue, looked in my eyes, and spoke to John in Polish, "There is a break in the lifeline— it is the war—and fortune has no control over the war. If he lives through the war, he will have a long, good life. Do not be afraid, his fortune line is very strong. "

Then she told John his fortune, while I walked over to my jacket pocket for one and a half packages of Lucky Strike cigarettes, rumored to be worth seventy-five dollars in "barter land." Neither John nor I ever smoked, so we were barter-rich. As soon as she was finished with John, we returned to our company, where John gathered together enough K rations—flour, coffee, tea, powdered milk, powdered eggs, etc.—to make the old girl rich for life. He also gave her two five-gallon cans of cooking fuel along with a two-burner stove. She looked like a little old grandmother, and maybe John thought she looked like his.

Borrowing a pickup truck from the motor pool, we rounded up all of the cigarettes that certain men owed to us, amounting to six and a half cartons of Chesterfields and Lucky Strikes. When we drove up to her little campsite and began off-loading the stuff into the back of her caravan, she and John took turns crying and hugging each other. John was calling her "Grandma" in Polish. When we explained that we really needed to return to our camp, she gave each of us a necktie that she said was a special Gypsy good luck charm that had been blessed, especially for us.

As we talked on our way back to camp, John was adamant about her power and through the years I have accepted his wisdom. In any case, it was late and we didn't take the time to check out our sleeping trench. We just assumed the two cooks had done a good job, especially since they were making the trench for their top kick and head cook.

We hit the sack at about 9:15 p.m. and the rain started at about 11:30. The sound of the rain dripping from the apple trees was very restful. However, the water started to run down the trench's gravel-wall sides into our sleeping arrangement. John awoke first, punching me in the back and telling me to wake up. "You Irish bastard. It's bad enough that it's raining, but you stink. I thought you took a bath. You really smell bad."

I said, "You shut the hell up. It's you who stinks." This argument went back and forth and we both agreed that something sure as hell smelled bad.

John said, "Get your damn hand the hell out of my face, you crazy, dumb, Irish numb nut."

I stood up and started to put my shoes on when John really started to get annoyed and told me to get my hand out of his face because it stunk so much it made him sick. "Povaznik," I said, "I have put my shoes on, here are my two hands," and I reached over with each hand on each of his shoulders. John was perplexed. I said, "Are you convinced, John? If I have two hands and these are my hands you owe me an apology. What are you dreaming about?" With that Sergeant Povaznik picked up his heavy-duty flashlight and turned the light into the area where his head had rested.

I don't know which one of us said, "Holy crap," but there was a hand and an arm leaning over and into where John's face had been. His pillow would now gag a skunk. I called for the sergeant of the guard to set up a tarpaulin over our sleeping trench and bring some trenching tools and torchlights.

We had found the body of a German soldier who, we were told later by the FFI, had been killed a few weeks ago and buried in the orchard, parallel to our trench. The FFI gave him a new military funeral, wrapped him in one of our body bags, and marked his grave carefully. We had to destroy the clothing and blankets that had been in the trench.

* * *

During World War II, censorship overseas was honed to a fine edge, trying to ensure that the enemy would not get wind of future troop movements. There was censorship of all service personnel mail, both incoming and outgoing. The job of censor was usually assigned to an officer, but sometimes a high-ranking noncom was chosen. That happened to me. I was assigned by the captain to help one of our platoon officers with his overload of outgoing mail.

When Sergeant Smith became aware that I was his censor and actually would be privy to all of his mail, he was extremely annoyed, especially since it was now my job to stop some BS types of weird remarks that he had written to his stateside lady friends. So for weeks he salted his mail with weird words and foolish promises—anything to aggravate his censor.

One rainy day, I hitched a ride to the different half-tracks' revetments with the mail jeep. I performed my chores, checking each track's fields of fire and their combat readiness. After I handed out the mail I proceeded to the next track's area of responsibility. When we were approaching Smith's track, I could see that he was royally annoyed. He couldn't stand still. He started to yell as he motioned for me to vacate the jeep fast. At the same time he kept waving a piece of paper in the air, obviously a letter.

When I was near enough to Smith, the knucklehead punched me on my arm and screamed that his best girl had finally answered his f****** letter. She had told him, in no uncertain terms, that if he couldn't write a letter to her without using his filthy army language, he need never waste her time with another one of his stupid, "sheety" letters. What made Smith angry was not what she had said, but that "the stupid bimbo" couldn't spell "shitty."

Joe had tried to explain in his letters to Florence (whom he now called "sheethead") that we had seen so much action, it was clearly not a question of if he would get hit, but when. He had also told her that when he did get hit he would be hit bad.

I looked at Smith for a solid minute and said, "Joe, you two 'sheety' people were made for each other. Don't give her up!"

The rain had slowed down to a slight drizzle and Joe and his crew had pretty much filled up their helmets with rainwater so that they could wash, rinse and then honor Joe's twenty-third birthday. Incidentally, if exposure to driving rain doesn't count, we had been unable to wash for the last two weeks. To be a wise ass Joe was standing before his crew at parade rest, so I took the time to look Smith and his crew over. They were well-trained soldiers with a lot of combat experience. Smith was five feet ten and a half inches tall and weighed about 156 pounds. Of course a lot of that weight was dirt and mud. He was dirty. He smelled dirty. When he raised his arms to signal the crew, they would all yell, "Put your arms down, please."

Joe's helmet had two big dents on one side from shrapnel. He was also definitely out of uniform. He was wearing a very smelly Yankee sweatshirt cut off at the elbows, with numerous food tracks caked on his belly. His boots were covered with mud and his hands and arms were covered with scratches caked with blood. He was a mess, but there was still that certain stance that said, "I am a combat soldier." And his weapons—a .45 caliber side arm and a liberated German P-38 in a shoulder holster—were very, very clean.

Sergeant Joe gave me one of his f\*\*\*-you looks, kind of grinned and asked, "Well, what the hell would you do, Top, if you had received a letter from a female that can't spell 'doggy doo'?"

I gave him the answer he wanted to hear. "Joe, to hell with her. Even with your stinking odor and your filthy dirty clothes and muddy shoes, you're still one of the best-looking sergeants in the ETO. She will be a sorry 'sheet' someday when she finds out that not only are you brave and a hero, but that someday you will be given a GI bath by your crew."

Joe laughed, raised his "everybody shut the hell up" arm, and told me I was wanted by battalion headquarters. Scram!

* * *

The question most asked of a sergeant about his soldiers is "Will they fight if there is a battle?" My answer always was, "Yes, they are proud of their buddies and they will never abandon their obligations."

As usual the weather was miserable, the dampness penetrating. The wind was still blowing over the top of our hill and cold as hell. I was wearing my new field jacket that Dad had sent to me when we were still in England. Sergeant Smith was quick to point out how dumb I was to wear a clean jacket to a possible firefight. I would stand out as a conspicuous target, he said.

Buck Sergeant Gargano, a guy of about standard size who had been with us since our basic training days, had picked up a BAR somewhere along the way, and had enough rounds to start another war of his own. He was on a constant search for enemy handguns, which he usually sent home to his dad or old friends. Those he did not send home he kept as personal side arms. This day he was wearing a Luger in a German shoulder holster and a German paratrooper's .46 caliber Mauser as a side arm.

I remember distinctly that Sergeant Gargano and his crew were with us on top of this damned hill. We were waiting for orders to join up with the rest of the battalion, at which point we would try to help protect the world-renowned Chartres Cathedral. It was in the center of the town, about four and a half miles from our hillside perch. Sergeant Gargano was bitching about the weather, the distance to town, and the fact that we would need to circumvent an SS noncom school. Rumors were that the school was equipped with sniper's rifles that could shoot around corners as well as bullets made of balsa wood. Trying to attack an NCO school was, to quote one of Sergeant Smith's witticisms, "equivalent to swimming head-on into a large school of big white starving sharks with your legs and feet bleeding."

One of the companies that had led the way into the town had been fired on by the SS men using the wooden bullets. The poor men hit were in a bad way. When the balsa wood penetrated an arm or a leg, it would soak the liquid from the blood, making it necessary to remove the extremity. Who said the palms of your hands don't sweat?

As we left the hill, I was leading a four-man patrol when a mortar round hit us. I was out front and the three men were fanned out and covering our rear. All three of them were standing up and were killed. I was bending over, trying to pick up my carbine, when I heard the round coming in. I had the impression of falling from a vast height, falling through an immense black void without the slightest sensation. I was awakened by the stinging of sweat in my right eye, which had been the nearest to the mortar burst. I remember wiping a sleeve across my face. I don't know how long I was blacked out, but it couldn't have been long. I came to feeling like there was a black void in my head and in my lungs. I seemed to be swimming toward a light from a deep depth.

I vaguely recall assisting the medics in searching for the remains of my men. I had been the lucky one and apparently sustained only a concussion. However, two days later I lost consciousness and was hospitalized for ten days.

During my period of semi-consciousness when I got to the hospital, I was later told, a couple of visitors passing through the hospital recognized me. They wrote to a man in my company that I tried to sell them a submarine that I kept under my cot. Obviously, I was out of it. But after several days in recovery, a doctor advised me that I was in pretty good shape. However, he recommended that I not have access to any weapons. I asked, "How in the hell do they think I can manage my combat company against combat Germans?" I won that argument.

One of the doctors dropped me off at my battalion, with a "Good luck and God bless." My guys gave me a royal welcome and my .45. We were on alert, and were billeted near the cathedral in protection mode for several days.

\* \* \*

Adolph Hitler wanted Paris defended to the last man. The city's seventy bridges were to be prepared for demolition. "Paris," Hitler ordered, "must not fall into the enemy's hands, except as a field of ruins."

The military commander of Paris was General of Infantry Dietrich von Choltitz. He had erected strong defenses outside the city, manned by about 20,000 troops. Another 5,000 troops remained inside the city. Fortunately, General Choltitz had no intention of seeing Paris destroyed. He loved its physical beauty as well as its cultural significance. He was appalled by the destruction he had been ordered to unleash. Had fate selected him for infamy as the man who had destroyed the French capital? He hoped not.

He explained to his superiors that he had placed three tons of explosives in the Cathedral of Notre Dame, two tons in the Invalides, and one in the Palais Bourbon. He was ready, he said, to level the Arc de Triomphe and clear a field of fire. He was ready to destroy the opera house and the Madeleine Church. He told them he planned to dynamite the Eiffel Tower and use it as an entanglement to block the Seine. He had no intention of doing any of these things, but he hoped that what he said would not only appease his superiors but also keep the French resistance inside the city in check.

General de Gaulle had organized the Resistance outside France to support his provisional government. But inside France, and particularly in Paris, a large and vociferous contingent of the left contested de Gaulle's leadership. De Gaulle had named General Marie Pierre Joseph Francois Koenig head of the Resistance in France and placed him under Eisenhower's command. Rumors of civil unrest in Paris and talk of a liberation initiated by the inhabitants prompted Koenig to try to stop activities that might cause social and political upheaval. A revolt in Paris might provoke bloody repression by the Germans. A bloody insurrection could place de Gaulle's enemies in power. Civil disorder might grow into full-scale revolution.

Despite Koenig's efforts, the approach of American troops provoked patriotic excitement within the city. By August 18, more than half of the railroad workers were on strike and the city was at a standstill. Virtually all of the policemen had disappeared from the streets. Anti-German demonstrations took place and armed resistance members appeared openly. General Choltitz decided to surrender Paris.

Actually, plans for the liberation of Paris had started long before the invasion of Normandy. In 1943 the Allies had listed a French division among the units earmarked to travel from England to the continent, primarily so there would be a major French formation present at the reoccupation of Paris. The second French Armored Division was selected for the task. General Dwight D. Eisenhower, as supreme Allied commander, promised to use the division to liberate the capital.

The division commander was Major General Philippe Francois Marie de Hautecloque, an aristocrat and thorough patriot. Known as "Leclerc," he had served as a regular army captain during the 1940 campaign. After the French surrender, he made his way to England and joined General de Gaulle. Headstrong and impatient, Leclerc burned with desire to erase the shame of the French defeat. De Gaulle sent him to Africa and Libya. Attached to Lieutenant General Bernard Montgomery's Eighth Army, he fought on its left flank. In the process, Leclerc advanced rapidly in rank and gained a legendary reputation.

Having functioned in Africa more or less independently, he was ill suited to the discipline of the chain of command. Toward the end of 1943, de Gaulle instructed Leclerc to form the Second French Armored Division. Leclerc pulled the division together from diverse sources. It contained Free French from the United Kingdom as well as soldiers from Syria, French North Africa, and equatorial Africa. They were Catholics, Protestants, Jews, Muslims, and animists, but they seemed to get along with each other, as did the Communists, Socialists, free thinkers, militant Christians, and Quakers among them. They had the exuberance of freebooters, and they were bound together by their hatred of the Germans, their love of France, and their loyalty to Leclerc.

On August 1, 1944, almost two months after D-Day, the Second French Armored Division arrived in Normandy at Omaha Beach. It was to be part of Lieutenant General George Patton's Third U.S. Army. Patton needed units and he called Leclerc in for a talk. Patton offered Leclerc the opportunity to go into battle immediately instead of waiting to liberate Paris. According to Patton, the Germans were about to surrender. If Leclerc wanted to fight, he had better get started.

Leclerc jumped at the chance. Patton put Leclerc and his division into the XV Corps, commanded by Major General Wade Hampton Haislip. A well-heeled Virginian, he had been a student at the Ecole de Guerre, the war college in Paris. Patton and Haislip both spoke French fluently. They welcomed Leclerc and tried to make him feel at home.

On August 15, Leclerc went to see Patton and found General Bradley with him. Both generals assured Leclerc that he would have the honor of liberating Paris when the time came. These promises did not assure General Leclerc. He knew American troops were closer to Paris than he was. In fact, my half-tracks were closer to Paris than his were, since we had cleared the back roads. His division's half-tracks were back at Chartres. If Eisenhower had to liberate Paris quickly, an American contingent would be able to reach Paris sooner than Leclerc.

Of course General Patton would have loved to liberate Paris himself. The city knew how to welcome heroes, and Patton's sense of theatrics certainly would have enlivened the festivities. Unlike most Allied officers, Patton had a real love of France and the French. His relations with the French leaders—Charles de Gaulle, Alphonse Juin, Pierre Koenig, and Leclerc—were excellent.

In any event, on the evening of August 21 Leclerc sent about 150 men in light tanks, ten half-tracks, ten armored cars, and ten personnel carriers toward the capital. Our half-tracks were to reconnoiter the routes to Paris. If and when anyone asked, we were to make it clear that Paris had been liberated through the strength of "Allied arms." General Eisenhower planned to march the 28th Infantry Division through Paris to their front on August 29. The 28th Division made its way through the city. Eisenhower, Bradley, Gerow, de Gaulle, Koenig and Leclerc reviewed the parade from an improvised platform, an upside-down Bailey Bridge. Eisenhower had invited Montgomery to attend but the British general said he was "too busy."

As they became aware of the Allied role in liberating France, Parisians came to acknowledge and to understand the American presence in the liberation of their city. They seem to have decided that only very good friends could share that privilege, so it was all right for the Americans to be there. American soldiers were greeted warmly by Parisians. The most affectionate welcome, however, was reserved for the men of the Second French Armored Division, many of whom were returning to their homes after more than four years of exile.

My unit reached Paris early, with our two half-tracks totally primed for action. At noon on August 23, I turned my two half-tracks over to General Leclerc in front of the Hotel de Ville. As the bells of nearby Notre Dame began to ring joyously, another church took up the refrain and then another. Soon all the churches in Paris were ringing their bells in celebration. The cascade of sound could only mean one thing. The liberators had arrived. It was bedlam.

On the following morning, August 24, the official day of liberation, an enormous crowd of joyous Parisians welcomed the arrival of the Second French Armored Division. Paris had been returned to the

French! Smith, Gargano, Felix, and Rex Kaufman insisted we have our pictures taken in front of the Eiffel Tower. We plowed through the happy, bumping, kissing, hugging crowds on our way there. At one point, Staff Sergeant Lou Danuicci stumbled and tripped, put his arms around Gargano, and gave him a big hug and kiss, barely missing as he did this a Parisian with a bottle of wine. Later Gargano insisted that the only reason he stayed boozed up for the rest of the day was that a scary big man had hugged him, and Gargano did not want nightmares called Sergeant Lou.

After taking a slew of pictures in front of the Eiffel Tower (along with a few hundred people with the same idea) we made our way back to our assigned hotel, walking past Notre Dame Cathedral and along the River Seine on the right bank, finally reaching the Rue de Rivoli just before midnight. The bells were still ringing in many of the churches. As we entered the hotel, we were ushered across the lobby by two men, both of whom spoke perfect English, telling us that they were at our total beck and call during our stay at the hotel and in Paris.

Paris was lit up like New York's Times Square on New Year's Eve. So, in fact, were most of its inhabitants! The wild celebration had continued all day. We were having sandwiches and wine on our balcony when Gargano needed the john. Hearing a bloodcurdling yell and gushing water, we rushed inside to find one wet pissed-off Gargano, who had just been introduced to a bidet.

The celebration continued outside our windows all night, and true to their promise, the two ushers tapped on our doors at 6:45 a.m. with our uniforms cleaned and pressed. When we attempted to pay them, they asked for a couple of cigarettes, any type. I walked over to my gas mask container and gave each man a pack of Lucky Strikes. They told us that a pack of unopened cigarettes in France cost fifty dollars.

After taking our breakfast orders, they again refused our money. We all went to our gas mask holders and gave them what the two ushers considered a fortune in barter material. When asked if there was a barbershop in the hotel, the big usher nodded his head and said, "The best." Pierre returned to our room at 9:30 to usher me to the barber's. The barbershop was a palace and my barber spoke Spanish,

English and French. Thank the Lord I was clean. My usher left and my barber started cutting what we called an "Army short cut." The barber asked if I would like to have a shave and a manicure. It seems the ushers had told the barber not to charge me for any work. I told the barber that he was the first man ever to give me a shave, and the girl holding my hand was definitely giving me the first manicure I had ever had.

We had been alerted that by 1200 we were to return to our convoy behind Notre Dame, to return to Third Army Zone. By the time our group reached the area of our convoy, most of the truck drivers had started mingling with the Parisians who crowded around the trucks. Lots of wine and booze was being shared. Of course, my squad joined in. That definitely included me. Special MPs were trying, without much success, to maintain some semblance of order. One of them with an apparent dislike of first sergeants must have spotted my stripes. He gave me one helluva whack above my knee.

I passed out, my guys threw me into the back of the truck, and that was the last I saw of Paris.

# 7

# FROM PARIS TO THE RHINE

After I woke up, I learned our orders had been changed. Our convoy was moving south towards Chartres, where our battalion was to regroup. My first priority was to replace the two half-tracks I had turned over to Leclerc. We were also low on supplies, including ammo.

What was supposed to be a brief respite dragged on for weeks. Fuel and supplies were slow in arriving. Even the Red Ball express was not getting through. During this period, weather conditions changed suddenly. Cold rains and winter weather came early that fall.

We were finally refitted, half-tracks and all, and ready to move out to make a major thrust toward the Rhine. Our half-tracks towed 40mm cannons as antiaircraft protection for the Third Army's infantry. We soon discovered the Germans had also reinforced their lines of defense, and the rain, sleet and hail were a real deterrent. The advance was slow. We had to fight hard for each hill and village. It was grim, dirty work, and we soon found ourselves low on supplies as well. The advance halted.

Thank the good Lord, orders were handed to me stating that we were to have a forty-eight-hour equipment repair period at the Third Army repair center, followed by a seventy-two-hour rest period. It was about time. The whole damned battalion was exhausted, certifiably shell-shocked and battle weary. Patton did his best looking after his men, making sure we got regular mail, the best available food, a daily change of socks to prevent trench foot, hot showers, and clean clothes.

Finally we were on the move again. During the next five weeks in November and December we fought in depressing conditions resembling the battle of the hedgerows in Normandy. The rain was constant. Again ammunition supplies remained low. We heard we had a shortage of riflemen and were in need of good replacement troops. Frustrated with logistical and personnel deficiencies, Patton supposedly remarked, "At the close of the war, I intend to remove my insignia and wristwatch. But I will continue to wear my short coat so that everyone can kiss my ass."

By December 15 we had advanced about forty miles in heavy fighting. We were well on our way to the Rhine. Then, on December 16, all hell broke loose. Up north the Germans opened their Ardennes counteroffensive. Within a week we were among the troops rerouted north and were dug in somewhere near Stuith. The miserable weather continued—snow and freezing, slippery ice.

One night, I had spread out my shelter half against a caved-in stone wall and covered my body with my overcoat. My legs and feet felt like frozen, aching, useless blocks of ice. It was about 2300 hours when Sergeant Smith nudged me awake and whispered, "Quiet!" Off in the woods we could hear the squeaking of large tanks, without a doubt German Tiger tanks. Smith claimed that the tank crews were all singing "Lili Marlene," their voices loud and slurred. They were drunk!

We received orders from headquarters to install two grenades on our guns' breechblocks and get the hell out of there! But—go where? We stuck it out. By the grace of God there was no engagement, that time.

The intense fighting continued through the holidays and the weather remained awful. Everybody was cold and tired. Eventually we heard that the Germans, after sustaining heavy losses, had extricated themselves from the Bulge and moved back to regroup. Once again we were on the move. Throughout February the weather was rotten. Moving along roads that had been destroyed, progress was slow as we headed south.

\* \* \*

Our antiaircraft battalion used complicated electrical equipment in the field. Our 40mm's were controlled by an electric-director that was serviced by an engineer, as were our half-tracks that fired four .50 caliber machine guns. Therefore it was necessary to have an expert electrician available and on call whenever heavy guns had a misfire or some other malfunction.

Our electrician was "Master Sergeant Permanent Rank Jakes." Sergeant Jakes had been a master sergeant for a long time, having earned his buck sergeant stripes during World War I. As a permanent rank, he could not lose any stripes except by an act of Congress. I remember the first time I met him. He was wearing his many ribbons plus awards, including two Purple Hearts and awards for bravery earned during the Mexican expedition of 1916 and World War I. His six-month service stripes had been modified into a special five-year stripe by act of Congress. They were worn only by soldiers who had served with honor in the U.S. Army during the Mexican expedition and World War I—the "war to end all wars."

Sergeant Jakes had spent a lot of time with our company before we had left for Europe. He seemed to have adopted my Company D, making sure that our directors and guns were in perfect condition. I think he was impressed with Sergeant Smith's insistence on perfection and his crew's performance. Whatever his reasons, due in no small part to his attention to our equipment, whenever there was a battalion inspection Sergeant Joe Smith's weapons were judged as exceptionally maintained and combat ready.

Sergeant Jakes was well-known in the upper echelons of the army because of his permanent rank and many awards. Both were very rare. He was allowed in many combat zones and had perfected the "Golden Rule" of sergeants—never being operationally short in the field. Anything that he "found" abandoned and he could use was his. In a combat area, he was a work of art.

One morning he showed up at Sergeant Smith's gun crew, riding a German motorcycle with an American sidecar. Our American nuts did not work with German bolts, so he had used a length of heavy-duty wire to tie the American sidecar in a half-assed hookup to the German motorcycle. I was nearly finished with my inspections of the different gun crews, and Sergeant Jakes offered to speed up my inspection by driving me in his sidecar to the last two revetments.

Sergeant Jakes mounted his motorcycle and while I was squeezing my body, jacket, .45 automatic and carbine into the sidecar, I noticed Jakes was putting an MP's brassard on his arm and when he saw me looking, he told me that he was an honorary military policeman. Then he pushed down the gas pedal and with a jerk we were off, wheels spinning. The two wheels on the motorcycle were fine, but my wired sidecar wheel pulled loose. He went left while the sidecar moved right about eight yards and started to spin like a top. When I finally stopped spinning, he was laughing like a jackass.

When we got back to battalion, he had to tell everybody, including the colonel. The colonel laughed until he had tears in his eyes, saying *Stars and Stripes* should be advised, which he did!

\* \* \*

A week after the Battle of the Bulge, our battalion had been shipped back to Cambrai, France, near the Belgium border, to repair equipment, get new uniforms, and best of all take R and R for two weeks—with hot showers.

Early one Saturday morning Sergeant Jakes arrived and parked his motorcycle near our company's headquarters. As luck would have it, I was just leaving a meeting in my captain's office and bumped into him. I followed him out to his cycle, where he proceeded to talk me into going back to the Ardennes to see if we could find a wrecked or abandoned jeep. Jakes admitted that he couldn't use his sidecar but said that his motorcycle was in pretty good shape.

The next morning when he picked me up he had a five-gallon can of gas strapped over the rear wheel. Jakes had "borrowed" a parked jeep's jerry can. I was to use it as a cushion during our long trip, about sixty-five miles each way over very rough roads full of potholes from strafing planes. We had traveled about twenty bumpy, very sore-ass miles when I started to yell for Jakes to stop. The combined weight of the fuel can and me were too much. We had a slow leak in the rear tire.

Sergeant Jakes had an idea. We would remove the gas can and pour most of the gas into the motorcycle's tank, then throw the gas can away. He suggested I take my jacket off, fold it up and sit on it. Maybe if we drove fast enough the tire wouldn't lose any more air.

This time we only went only about six miles when it became obvious that the rear tire was too soft to continue with both of us on the cycle. He suggested that I stay put while he continued to the Ardennes and see what he could find around Malmedy. As soon as he found a functioning jeep and fixed the cycle's tire, he would return. I would then drive the jeep and he his motorcycle back to our company's area. A very simple plan.

Sergeant Jakes handed me one of his MP brassards and told me: "Wear it. Don't take any crap from anyone. Relax. Don't leave the road and I will be back for you as soon as I find an operational jeep. Remember, this road will take you back to our battalion if you have to hitchhike back." Then he put his leg over his bike, checked his throttle, and yelled over the noise: "If I can't find a driveable jeep in two hours of searching, I will get a new rear tire or a patch for the cycle and pick you up in about seven or eight hours. If you are not on this road I will assume that you hitched a ride, and I will see you tomorrow. Don't wait too long, because if it gets dark, I will have trouble finding you." With that, he was off.

I spent the time sitting on a large log by the side of the road, jumping out of the way of some jackass drivers in empty trucks, on their way back to Normandy to pick up loads of gas for Patton in the Ardennes.

Hours later, Jakes came back up that pockmarked shot-up road, swerved slowly then pulled over. He told me that he had taken a few bypass roads back to the international area and got his rear tire repaired. His trip had been very productive. He reached into his sidesaddle and brought out three canteens, one of wine and two of coffee, saying the wine was for the end of our trip. He then produced four sandwiches of ham and cheese plus a very clean towel.

Jakes said he was a bit worried about me making it back on the cycle. But, he said, there was a very large house about a mile and a half down the road that sported a soldier walking a guard post and a jeep that was parked in the middle of the guard's post. We were going to borrow that jeep. "Put your MP armbands on and follow my lead!"

I looked at the rear tire of Sergeant Jakes' motorcycle before swinging my leg over a new jerry-gas-can rear seat. I said a prayer and said, "Let's go!"

We had bounced a short mile when Jakes told me that our object was dead ahead and for me to let him do all of the talking. Sergeant Jakes very carefully steered his cycle up close to the jeep and told me to wait for his directions. Then he motioned for the guard to approach him, and for me to examine the jeep. It was obviously in very good condition. As Sergeant Jakes pointed to his MP armbands and stopped the guard from walking his post by the jeep, he informed him that the jeep was breaking "U.S. Army Traffic Rules." It was illegally parked on this main highway leading to Normandy's off-loading port. "This is General Patton's main route for moving the gas for his tanks to the Red Ball express," he said. "It has to be removed. I will hand you a receipt for the location, recovery and fine, OK?"

The guard said, "Thank you. But according to my sergeant, we are responsible for only the house, not the jeep." Sergeant Jakes was annoyed at this, but happiness was quickly restored. First we found a heavy steel chain was locked through the steering wheel of the jeep and then double chained on the bottom of the passenger's seat brace. But Jakes laughed and showed the guard that the key to the lock was hanging from the windshield wiper. While the guard removed the key and chain, Sergeant Jakes took one of the MP armbands from my arm and gave it to the kid, with a warning: "Don't flash it, send it home to your mother." He then wrote up a phony letter to cover the kid's ass, saying that the jeep was taken to help out in an emergency. We shook hands and left, me driving the jeep, Jakes in front of me on the cycle.

We stopped immediately, on the road in front of the large house, to see if perhaps there might be an old trip ticket anywhere in the jeep.

A trip ticket is what a motor pool sergeant issues to an authorized soldier allowing him to operate and utilize the assigned vehicle. That's when Jakes and I walked over to the sign posted on the front lawn. It said, "Property of SHAEF." I was sitting in the driver's seat of Ike Eisenhower's jeep!"

We took off, with Sergeant Jakes ahead of me but behind two large tank trucks on their way back to Normandy to refuel. We came to a checkpoint and I could see the drivers hand over their trip tickets to be stamped as OK to pass into the "international territory," which was about two city blocks in length. At night the territory was well lit by large power lights. At the end of each block there were railroad gates that were lowered and raised by the guards as trip tickets were submitted and validated.

As I came to my first gate, I watched Sergeant Jakes pass through it without incident. Given his personal motorcycle's trip ticket and the master sergeant's MP band on his arm, General Patton himself couldn't have waved him down.

That didn't help me. I pulled up to the closed gate and two mean-looking tech sergeants asked to see my trip ticket. I began to search all over the jeep for the nonexistent trip ticket, as did both guards. After a few wasted minutes during which the trucks and tankers in line behind me began blowing their claxon horns for attention, the guards motioned for me to pull over into a small parking lot. I had visions of a few months in Leavenworth Prison. But as I started to get out of the jeep, I heard Sergeant Jakes returning on his cycle. He started giving the two guards hell and yelled that the jeep was being escorted by him, and for them to get the hell out of the way or he would ticket them for holding us up.

Jakes took off and they waved for me to follow him. As I pulled the jeep out of the small parking lot they gave me a salute! Driving down the street I had the weird feeling that one or both of them were zeroing rifles in on the back of my head. When I reached the number two gate Jakes was waiting for me and we made a clean exit. Yet I still had one hell of a feeling that somebody might just take a little target practice on the back of my head.

We got back to our battalion area about 3 a.m., dead tired. Jakes went off to his sack. I parked our new jeep and dragged my sore ass up the three flights to my attic sack and went out like a light. At 5:30 a.m. the sergeant of the guard was shaking me awake with the words, "The captain wants you in his office at once." I still had my traveling clothes on so I threw some water in my face and I was on my way.

The captain was visibly annoyed. "We've obviously got brass on board. Their jeep is parked behind your half-track. Find out where the hell they are. Get on it right away!"

I left and phoned Jakes. "Get your butt over here and meet me behind the track—pronto." Shortly after I got there, Jakes' cycle roared in next to me. I greeted him with, "Get rid of the jeep or we are in deep s***! The captain thinks brass from SHAEF is nosing around the area and he's hot to know what's going on. If he discovers we're involved, we're history. You've gotta get rid of the jeep."

Jakes laughed and said, "Forget about it, numb nuts. I'll handle it." He took off in the jeep. I again dragged my ass up three flights of stairs to my cot and sleep.

About 2 p.m., I was awakened by Jakes, standing in the doorway and grinning from ear to ear, with a bottle of Three Feathers whiskey in each hand. He sat down on my three-legged chair and announced, "Mission accomplished. I drove the jeep over for breakfast at the NCO Club and damned if the colonel wasn't there with his talkers on. When he ran out of steam, I asked how he was set for wheels. That elicited a diatribe about how bad the situation was, and how everything was in short supply. He went on and on about broken axles, windshields, until I realized he hadn't understood me. So I said, "Colonel, how would *you* like a new jeep with no questions asked?"

That's how Jakes had ended up with a case of Three Feathers. Sometime later, Jakes told me that while the guys were cleaning the jeep for delivery to the colonel, they discovered a different set of ID numbers under SHAEF's insignia. That jeep had really been around!

I reported to the captain that the SHAEF problem had been resolved. No brass was located in the area, and the jeep had been returned. Depositing a bottle of Three Feathers on his desk, I was dismissed. With a wink. Of course it was well-known that he had a bad eye.

\* \* \*

It was not unusual for combat groups to find abandoned enemy weapons or vehicles. After carefully checking these vehicles for booby traps and repainting the identity emblems, a driver would be assigned and we would have a new addition to what was called our "gypsy army." Dog Company's gypsy army at one time or another consisted of two German tanks and a Volkswagen. We chopped a hole in the roof of the VW so that passengers could stand up and fire a BAR or a machine gun from the hole.

Our company was directed to take over Field Marshal Herman Goering's hunting lodge. When we arrived we discovered the lodge was actually a textbook example of a castle—a "fortified dwelling for nobility." It had a moat and a large inner court. Built on top of a mountain, there was an impressively steep sheer drop on its backside.

Best of all, a carriage house held four very expensive cars, all up on concrete blocks, with no gasoline in their tanks. We proceeded to fill the tank of a Mercedes-Benz touring car, in perfect condition, and added it to our gypsy army. There were even a few weapons in a special carrier under the rear seat. We drove the touring car a few hundred miles before the war's end, without a single dent.

Nothing brought our men more happiness than our small German tank, even though we ran out of 88mm shells within four days after we found it. The driver sat in the seat with two brake handles. When you pulled on the left brake handle, the left tread stopped while the right tread continued to run, turning the tank to the left—and vice versa. Whenever Sergeant Smith was at the controls he loved to spin the tank like a top. He was dangerous as hell, driving it like a carnival car, not a weapon.

We were very careful with it at every crossroad, however. Usually we asked Felix to speed across the intersection in our VW, with some noncom's head and shoulders peeking out of the hole in its roof.

Shouting like a drunken Indian, he would fire one of our captured machine guns in every direction, hoping that would distract any enemy in the vicinity.

\* \* \*

Our captain complained constantly that he was "going mad, slowly but irrevocably mad." The worst part of that, he said, was that his actions *were* those of a madman. He wasn't alone in worry about how the war had changed him.

I knew if I were able to look into a mirror, there would be new lines under my eyes, deeply etched, and I would see the hair at my temples turning white. My hands traveled over my face; I could feel a three-week growth of grungy beard. I didn't want to look at my clothes. I knew they were dirty, soiled and stained due to a nervous sweat from too much stress. Sergeant Joe was always busting my gonads about getting old and ugly. Joe's favorite comment was, "With a shave and a good night's sleep, you might pass for fifty to sixty years of age."

Sergeant Joe had a cough that bit into his lungs constantly, a condition that wasn't helped by his sleeping on damp frozen ground for the past two years or by smoking a couple packs of Camels every day. I remember one night he was acting as our cook, heating up hot dogs and beans with cold biscuits. What he did was start up one of our half-tracks. Then, after washing out our iron helmets, he put food in them and placed them on the track's block with the hood down. After twenty or thirty minutes, we had warm meals.

Sergeant Joe hadn't washed for a couple of weeks. His helmet had two dents on one side, from pounding different objects. Every once in a while he would lose control and just slam his helmet on the hard ground. This time a couple of his crew reported to me that "Sergeant Joe was an SS guard, no matter what uniform he wore. He was too dirty, smelly and he was trying to destroy our half-track." I explained that Joe was making our lunch on the track, and I told the complaining buddies that Joe's odor was permanent.

\* \* \*

Patton's Third Army finally reached the Rhine River on March 7, near Coblenz. All the bridges had been destroyed and no immediate crossing was possible. Finally crossing at Remagen, Patton immediately fulfilled a promise he'd made to Hitler by pissing in the Rhine. He was annoyed when he later learned that Churchill and his escorts had urinated in the Rhine the previous day.

During the next two weeks we pushed on, clearing the western bank from Coblenz to Mannheim. Crossing the river at Oppenheim there had been minimal opposition, but when we were finally engaged we saw heavy action.

\* \* \*

A couple of our half-track crews had been able to make some good Tennessee home-recipe champagne and sherry. A few other crews were making a powerful Brooklyn-Bronx home brew from Rhine grapes. In addition, many soldiers had been eating grapes, plums and other fruits they had picked on the Rhine slopes. Many of them were getting the runs and messing their shorts. I thought that all ranks were going to need a first-aid station very soon.

\* \* \*

The essence of the story that follows is true. The incidents I describe all happened, but some of the details may be wrong. I kept a small diary and could refresh my recollections, but not completely. After fifty years, one's memory is fallible.

I knew we were off our GI maps when the road we were on paralleled an old barge canal that meandered back and forth to various old barge tollhouses. We were working our way up the Rhine, checking all large farms for the enemy. We were also checking roads into small villages that could harbor snipers, booby traps, or land mines.

Sergeant Carter had taken over Sergeant Russo's half-track following a close call Russo's half-track had had with a couple of snipers. Russo had gone off looking for some hair-raising German mortars that seemed to be coming from a barge tied up next to a destroyed bridge. He knew Carter's crew would utilize stealth while keeping alert for the very dangerous German snipers, some of them children, reported to be hanging about the small villages. Their assignment was to eliminate the enemy still holed up in the small villages along the Rhine, clearing the way for General Patton. At one point, they were missing, as far as I was concerned, on the other side of the Rhine.

I contacted Lieutenant Viola at battalion via our phone, reporting our situation. I told him we were heading up a north road. He authorized our trip with a "Go with God."

I was driving the Volkswagen with the hole chopped in the roof. Sergeant Gargano and two machine guns were in the back seat. Gargano also had with him his extra German grease gun, a very fast light German machine gun, his .45 automatic, and a shoulder-holstered Luger. I told him to signal to Sergeant Smith to follow us north. We were going to look for Carter and his crew.

It was a beautiful day, and I thought that by the end of the afternoon we would end a successful search for Carter. The other side of the Rhine's high mountains were ripe with the early bloom of grape vines. On our side, there were many small villages that supported strings of cafés. However, many had been in harm's way, blown up as the enemy withdrew to the north, and we knew many had been booby-trapped. Most of the bars had their doors and front windows smashed.

We had just passed a large winery when Gargano yelled in my ear, "There's Russo's half-track behind the winery."

I hit my brakes and Smith's half-track driver damned near creamed my Volkswagen. I cradled my Tommy gun and yelled to Smith, "Stay alert. Gargano and I are going to give a fast check and see what has happened to Carter's crew." Gargano automatically primed a grenade, something that always scared me because I was never sure who he was pissed at, us or the enemy.

As we entered the winery it was evident that what little of it hadn't been destroyed had been stolen. At the end of our inspection we paused to get our breath. We stepped outside to look at the very tall mountain that rose at the back of the building. Still on the lookout for Carter, Gargano offered to hike a few long yards up the side of the mountain to see what could be seen from there. Not seeing anything, he started back down and stumbled upon a double door that was virtually hidden near the foot of the mountain. It was very thick. Gargano took my Tommy gun and flashlight and pushed on one side with his foot. It fell from its hinges and tripped Gargano, who let out a loud Italian "pasta fazzoo."

When he stood up, we entered what turned out to be a hollow mountain, filled with row upon row, case upon case of different types of wines, stacked nearly to the ceiling. There were cases of schnapps, champagne, vodka, and both grape and plum wine. Then we came upon some man-sized barrels of German beer. There was one dimly lit light bulb hanging from an overhead beam. And under it, lying face-up, was Carter, passed out, along with two of his men, who had upchucked all over Carter.

A few feet from Carter's head there were a couple of man-size kegs that had been tapped, surrounded by a small lake of beer. Nearby was the remainder of Carter's crew, all soaking wet with red wine. Corporal Alex was sitting on an empty keg yelling, *"Oh* boy, I'm dying." Another of the crew was down on his knees praying, "Please, please take Alex and I'll go also!" The place reeked of beer, wine and vomit.

Suddenly, the drunks were interrupted by a loud, noisy yell of, "A-ten-hut," coming from the door we had entered. In came a chubby officer, obviously not a combat soldier. He yelled, "I am a provost marshal and I want to know who is in charge. Now, damn it, now, *now!"* He was obviously about to give me a real ass-chewing. I looked around at Gargano and the rest of my drunken, exhausted men, who had been pulling point for General Patton's Third Army for the last six weeks. I was about ready to yell, "I am in charge. These are my men. I am the SOB in charge of every one of them and I'm damned proud. My number is 32750111, you a-hole!"

Before I did, I heard another familiar voice. "What the hell is going on? You, Sergeant, I repeat, what the hell is going on? And you, Colonel, I'll talk to you later, after I speak to one of my combat sergeants. You, Sergeant Furgan? Your men have been on point, right?"

I said, "Yes, sir. We have been six weeks on your points."

General Patton said, "At ease," looked at me, then turned to the provost marshal and pointed to the door and barked, "Wait out there for me." Turning to me, he said, "We better get your men up and out in the air. Also, have your other crews load up your tracks with one case of their choice of champagne or wine—that's one case for each man. Then we will put a dial-lock and chains on this mountain until the end of the war, when we will have one hell of a party for the Third Army, hosted by General Patton and Sergeant Furkan."

He laughed and laughed, and said, "That's not how your name is pronounced, is it? Your name is Durkin, isn't it?" and he laughed again.

The next day, the crews were sipping some of General Patton's gift. The hell of it was, as soon as one of the men had even a drink of water, he was drunk all over again.

We ran into General Patton a few more times. He always pointed and laughed, and gave our half-track a wave.

# 8

# DACHAU

It was August 28, 1945. We were using our speed and armor to chase and annihilate any and all German soldiers on the Autobahn, the super highway that ran through Germany with an exit ten miles past Munich. In other words, we were eliminating as best we could the snipers and ambushers who had been firing from the rolling hills that bordered both sides of the highway.

I received a radio message that we were to stretch out my company's half-tracks into a special combat alert, stretching about a quarter of a mile, utilizing the fire power of each half-track's four .50 caliber synchronized machine guns. Consequently, I would be covering Sergeant Smith's rear in a German weapons carrier whose cross identification had been painted over by our army's star. As we were doing this I got another radio call, this time from our captain. He never talked on the phone. He yelled. He yelled so loud this time that I could barely understand the jackass. His third attempt at relaying his message, although not clear, turned out to be one of the worst orders I ever received. "Sergeant, you are to bypass the Munich exit. You will proceed to the Dachau cutoff. I want you to set up in a combat-ready mode and wait for Charley Company as reinforcement, then proceed to the concentration camp—Dachau."

As we drove our half-track and jeep up to the front gate of the camp, Sergeant Joe pointed out the large statue of a spread eagle holding a wreath and a swastika, which hovered over the entrance. Printed on top of it were the words "arbeit macht frei" (work makes one free). We got there at 1420 hours. When my captain arrived with C Company's weapons, we moved our tracks up through the large "Gates to Hell," and entered the camp.

I got out of my track and walked up to the captain's jeep. Both he and his driver were throwing up. The corporal on the machine gun was crying.

As soldiers, we were accustomed to the odor of death, even the odor of many mutilated bodies left exposed on a battlefield after one or two days in the humidity and sun. But the odor that filled our nostrils now was indescribable, ghastly. It wafted like a very heavy, clinging damp fog in our noses. Along one side of one of the nearest buildings was one of the Nazi killing ditches, about twenty-five feet wide and as deep as a one-story building. It was filled with the rotting flesh of women, children and babies. Some were partially burned or split open. There seemed to be extra heads, legs, and arms. Parts of a woman were holding part of a child in her arms.

We learned later that SS guards had utilized prisoners to do the filthiest, dirtiest work and called them "kapos." If a kapo was too slow, the SS would kill him and pick a new kapo to replace him. Kapos had been burning the corpses prior to our arrival to hide the SS guards' infamy. We could see a barn-like building with its very large sliding doors wide open, exposing the corpses of children, men and women stacked like cords of wood to the ceiling. We were to discover that a few of the bodies were still alive, barely.

We came across two SS guards who had been killed by the very weak prisoners. Because of their lack of strength and weapons, they had kneaded the guards' eyes, mouths and throats until they had no resemblance to ever having been human.

While trying to comprehend all of this horror, I was approached by an SS guard. He walked me over to one of the dead SS guards. The SOB actually wanted me to shoot a couple of the prisoners because, he said in broken English, they were crazy murderers. I pulled my .45 and stuck it under his chin, determined to blow the SOB's head off of his shoulders. But my captain yelled at me, "Don't! He is not worth it. Let him rot in hell, 'cause he won't make it to heaven." I stopped.

Sergeant Joe Smith, covered by Corporal Alex, ran over to a big farm wagon and found it loaded with bloody, dead naked men and women, their arms and legs askew. He saw that, under the adults' bodies, three SS guards had been trying to hide the bodies of several small children that were cut into pieces. One of the guards made a move as though to pull a gun from under the bodies, and Sergeant Smith hit him with his carbine, knocking him cold. The rest of the guards were marched to a cell and locked in.

In the meanwhile, the SS guard Smith thought he had knocked cold suddenly rolled over and fired a half clip at our captain and his driver. Then he got up and ran into a large brick building that had been the commandant's office. Sergeant Smith ran to the front of the building and tossed in a grenade. He went inside after the explosion and saw the shattered pieces of the SS guard sprawled against naked corpses of men and women stacked against the wall. Sergeant Smith was one sick puppy. We could not stop him from crying and heaving.

All of this had taken place within the first hour of our arrival. It was no wonder that the inmates had turned on the guards when we Americans arrived at the prison. The prisoners had no weapons in the beginning, but spurred to super-human strength by the approach of our men and freedom, they banned together and attacked their keepers with their bare hands. They had been able to seize a few guns, knives and clubs this way.

We told the prisoners they were free men, but they could not leave the camp until after our medics arrived. Many of them were dying from malnutrition, malaria, typhoid, and gangrenous sores. They all had scabies, mites, and lice.

Prior to our entering the concentration camp, a few SS guards had shot prisoners so that they could exchange their uniforms for the rags of the prisoners. They hoped to be mistaken for prisoners and therefore not face a firing squad for their crimes against humanity. None of them got away with it.

Many of the prisoners had been doctors, lawyers, professors and teachers. Some had held high political offices. Most could write and speak a number of different languages. Consequently, we liberators were able to obtain many stories concerning their day-to-day existence—the threats of torture, slow death due to a lack of food, and cruelty from the SS guards, Gestapo, and kapos.

I told Sergeant Smith to find a prisoner who spoke English and was strong enough to be our guide around the camp the next day. I also told him to make sure that a platoon of our best men, well armed, would be ready at 0700 hours.

\* \* \*

The next morning, Sergeant Smith introduced one of the liberated prisoners to me. He had been a teacher of the English language, and he volunteered an eyewitness account of one of the many mass murders he had seen committed by two of the special SS units at Dachau. He broke down and wept as he told us:

"One family had lived in my town. The children went to school with my kids. Without screaming or weeping, the family followed the SS orders, removing their clothes, folding every piece neatly and putting them down in a neat pile. Undressed, they stood around as a family group, kissed each other, said their farewells and waited for a sign from another SS Nazi, who stood near the pit with a whip in his hand. During the twenty to twenty-five minutes that I stood near, I heard no complaints or pleas for mercy.

"They were a family of eight persons—a man and his wife, both about fifty years old, with their children. One was eight, another nineteen, and there were two grown daughters in their early twenties. An old woman with snow-white hair, the grandmother, was holding the one-year-old child of one of the daughters in her arms, singing to it and kissing the baby. The child was cooing with delight. The man and his wife were looking on with tears in their eyes. The father held the eight-year-old boy's hand, speaking to him softly and pointing to the sky as he stroked the boy's head. He seemed to be explaining something to the boy. Then the SS Nazi at the pit shouted an order to the Nazi near the family. He counted off about twenty persons, instructing them to go behind a large earth mound."

The professor stopped speaking, choked and wiped his eyes and continued softly. "The family was a part of that group of twenty. I walked around the mound of dirt and found myself confronted by a tremendous grave. People were closely wedged together and lying on top of each other, so that only their heads were visible. The pit was already two-thirds full. We estimated that the pit already contained more than one thousand bodies.

"I looked for the devil that did the shooting. He was an SS officer who sat on the edge of the narrow end of the pit. His shiny jackboots were dangling into the pit. He had a machine gun resting on his knees and he was smoking a cigarette. I turned my head as I heard a series of shots. I could not watch the devil at play."

We realized how short a time it had taken for all those people to be killed—the dead in the wagon, the bodies stacked like logs seven hundred or eight hundred in the pit. It took only a few minutes for two or three SS guards to do this.

We were combat soldiers, but we were human. Seeing one mutilated child would have made us sick. But walking past a pile of fifty or sixty children who had been shot in the face just a day or two earlier, I couldn't stop thinking that if we had only driven our half-tracks and jeeps a little faster these children might still be alive. I will always live with that memory. As I will remember the father pointing to the sky and maybe saying to his son, "In just a little while we will all meet in Heaven."

When we continued around the grounds, we saw naked bodies lying in rows, sprinkled with quicklime. There were so many bodies that the water table of the whole area was being contaminated. Even the bacteria count of the drinking water at the SS barracks had gone up to the danger level.

The professor kept relating the horrors he had managed to live through. "There was an elite guard commander of the camp named Josef Kramer," he said. "Kramer had instituted a graduated series of tortures. Naked men and women had been forced to parade for hours in winter rains, sleet, and snow. Other prisoners, fully clothed, had been locked into compounds with vicious dogs that had been deliberately starved. Vivisection of prisoners was common. SS Kramer kept an orchestra that would play for him while he watched children, torn from their mother's arms, burned alive.

"The gas chambers disposed of people on a daily basis. The false showers used cyanide-5 and took twenty to thirty minutes to kill many people at a time. Kapos with gas masks would then drag the bodies from the showers and extract gold teeth from them"

We went inside one of the incinerators. It held the remains of a partially burned body, a young girl about eight to ten years of age. The girl's father was hanging nearby from a large meat hook, the kind a butcher would use to hang a large animal. The professor explained: "The reason the father was hanging was that he had been questioned by the kapos about where his wealth was hidden. The kapo would push the steel gurney that held the child into the furnace, burning off her legs and making her scream. That would make him talk. And of course the louder she screamed the more it terrified those being made ready for torture. Their turn was next."

Our next stop was called "the interrogation rooms." The first two rooms we walked into were in the cellar. Each room was twenty feet by twenty feet and totally packed with baby and children's shoes. Farther down the hall we entered a room that held a large steel table that had leg irons and handcuffs on it. After a prisoner was cuffed, the Nazis used three spigots. One was hot water, the second was very hot water, and the third was nearly steam. Hoses were inserted into the rectum of the prisoner and the spigots turned on full force. Usually the force of the water would blow out the abdomen of the prisoner. The noise could be heard over much of the camp. This is what the SS wanted to accomplish—to terrify, really terrify.

While in this large room our guide indicated that very often a prisoner was cuffed, naked, to the table by a kapo who was equipped with many different-size whips made like cat-o'-nine-tails. Each whip had six large lengths of leather with sharpened jacks on its end, about twice the size of those steel jacks that young girls used to play with.

One of the whips was lying on the table, its wooden handle covered with dry, caked blood.

It was growing late and we all felt completely exhausted. We set up security while other outfits were arriving and settling in. As tired as we were, I don't think any of was able to sleep that night.

The following day, after other divisions had been brought into Dachau, we were moved out to return to combat. A very somber, subdued Company D of soldiers left that day, unable to comprehend man's inhumanity to man.

Dear God in Heaven, why?

# 9

# END OF THE WAR

The war officially ended on May 9, 1945. In the months following, we were all anxious about relocation. The main thing we were concerned about was how many "points" we had. Soldiers who were married with children were the luckiest ones. They had the points to go home first. The rest of us waited.

One day Dog Company finally hit the jackpot. We had been assigned control of a large railroad hotel near a major terminal. Trains had to stop running at 6 p.m., and the passenger cars were always packed. The passengers included former German soldiers trying to get home and German prisoners going back to Poland, Russia and France. Many were displaced people whose homes had been destroyed, bombed out, lonely souls with nowhere to go—destination unknown.

All but one of our officers had been sent to other companies or had gone home. The lieutenant who was left barely put in an appearance at the hotel, spending most of his time at his girlfriend's house. That left me in charge of both the hotel and troops.

I had everything of value belonging to the hotel owners moved to an eighth-floor room. I bolted the doors to the room, posted guards and notified the owners where their stuff was via the town's mayor. Next I received permission to advance Corporal Charles Corson, company clerk, to buck sergeant and Sergeant Lou Dinucci to tech sergeant.

It was decided that Sergeant Lou would be in charge of all trips, especially those to the wine factory on the other side of town. Also it was necessary that Lou drive over to battalion every other day to pick up our Army rations, plus extra rations for the poor forgotten travelers at the hotel.

Lou frequently returned with some type of extra equipment. He returned one day with a back seat cushion from some German general's plush four-door sedan that he fit into his jeep. That jeep was equipped with all sorts of things for Lou's own personal adventures, and no questions about them were allowed. Not that anybody in his right mind would have dared ask. Sergeant Lou was in the process of rebuilding our hotel's bar and restaurant with stuff he found in nearby restaurants and bars that had been nearly destroyed. I encouraged that, because it meant I knew where our guys were after dark.

There was a large prison, a converted concentration camp, on the north side of the village we were in that held many dangerous Gestapo, SS officers and German troops that were being held under penalty of death. Among them were the SS officers and troops who had murdered forty-seven medics at Malmedy and were being held for the U.S. Army's court. There were also guards from Dachau. These prisoners were considered the worst scum of the earth and, if they should ever escape, the most dangerous.

But the war was over. None of us were carrying loaded weapons, except for those assigned as sergeant of the guards.

One morning Sergeant Lou informed me that he had hired a local six-piece band and some of the men wanted to set up a couple of crap tables and poker games. Sergeant Joe okayed the party until 1 a.m. Our lieutenant was still not available. Lou and Joe were going to run "the best dance party and bar this side of New York City." At least that's what the sign said at chow time. But shortly after chow the stuff hit the fan!

A jeep parked in front of the hotel and a provost marshal got out of it. He entered Sergeant Corson's office and requested the officer of the day. Sergeant Corson started laughing and told the provost, "We don't have an OD." Unhappy with the laughter, the provost insisted that Charlie stand at attention and send a messenger to find an officer—any officer—at once.

Sergeant Corson's answer was, "I can't! Sir!"

"Why in the hell not?" demanded the provost.

"Because we don't have any officers," Charlie said. "They had enough points and they have all been shipped out."

It was then that I think the provost lost it. He ordered Corson, "Sergeant, you take me to your leader."

Sergeant Corson said, "Follow me, please."

When they entered the restaurant, Sergeant Lou and I were just about ready for our party. We were sitting at the new bar, which sported a couple of large barrels and one small barrel of beer. Sergeant Lou had just tapped-off a glass. I gave Lou the high sign and we both stood and saluted the officer. Lou tendered him a tankard of German beer. "Top, I do believe the heat of the day was a blessing," said the provost to me. "Will you please send someone to your parking zone and have them send in my driver? We will give him a beer and I will explain our problem."

He went on, "First Sergeant Durkin, as you may be aware, on the north side of this town I have a leaky prison, a very dangerous leaky prison. The prisoners are escaping into the forest at the rate of ten or twelve murderous prisoners a night, and it has to be corrected immediately." Since our officers had been transferred, the provost informed me that he was assuming command of our company. He also said that, since I had been in charge of a combat company, I should be familiar with the rules of combat. I would therefore be responsible as the "officer" in charge of a twenty-four-hour combat team.

I tried my best to talk our way out of the assignment. I explained to him that we had just received a very late aggregate collection of packages from home, and we were looking forward to a short rest period prior to our turning in our equipment and then preparing for the long trip home. Unfortunately, the provost had been a combat lieutenant colonel and was not receptive to BS from a first sergeant. He told me to issue sufficient ammo to the different platoons and prepare to move out.

Then he gave me an overlay map and a schematic drawing of the "stalag"—the prison—and told me that the troops currently in charge of security were not combat and were allowing the SS prisoners to escape, which was not acceptable. The provost looked at us and said, "That's the problem. Those guards are all fresh from the States, and they will not fire on the prisoners. It's been fifteen days since the original combat guards were in place and the prisoners were afraid to take chances. Now they are escaping across the Danube River and scaring the hell out of the farmers."

Now I understood and asked, "Sir, what can we do to help? We were only three miles from Malmedy when they shot forty-seven of our medics." These medics, who did not carry weapons, were on their way to the Bulge at the time. They could have saved many lives. Instead, they had been murdered by the SS.

I had Sergeant Joe fall the men out, while Sergeant Lou got weapons and ammo for everyone, along with transportation, combat ready. I asked the Provost to join us. He explained to the assembled men what the situation was in the stalag. He told them how, once free of the camp, the SS escapees were intimidating the residents in the area, demanding money, clothes and side arms.

We had an assignment that we all accepted. Our job was to make sure that no prisoner would escape, that the "ghosts of Malmedy" would be avenged if even one SS officer or man tried to escape. Any prisoner who tried to approach the first ditch inside the stalag and running on the inside of the barbed-wire fence would be considered totally out of bounds and should therefore be considered a target. Each of the three towers in the camp would be manned by a sergeant and two men with a sufficiency of .50 caliber ammo. They were authorized to shoot any prisoner that refused to stop moving toward the wire, after first firing a couple of rounds over their heads.

I assigned armed units to each tower and set up three eight-hour shifts. We posted our people that night.

The next day I questioned the sergeants and was relieved to hear that not one prisoner had reached the wire. However, our medics had gone inside the wire to treat ten prisoners who had refused to stop and were therefore shot by our men.

That afternoon I was alerted that the marching of prisoners around the periphery had become almost like a combat exercise. Consequently, at 0100 hours, I had Sergeants Sharpe and Smith fire up and arm their half-tracks, telling them to report to the provost marshal and me for combat orders as soon as they could. Upon their arrival I told Sergeant Sharpe to circle right and Sergeant Smith to circle left, each to modify their times of passage for safety.

Our tour ended at 0700. Four black body bags and six wounded were shipped to the medics. When we held our morning formation the next day, I turned the company over to the provost marshal, who said, "Your execution of this assignment has been exemplary. I do not believe there will be another escape from the prison. I hope you men arrive home for Christmas."

After that, Sergeant Lou and one of his cooks delivered a most welcome breakfast—with a surprise. There was a filled wine glass next to each plate of hotcakes and homemade German sausage. We could eat as much as we desired. The troops sat wherever they wished, and rehashed some of the scarier parts of what had happened in the stalag. As they finished eating, I stood up and blew my whistle for attention. They all stood at strict attention and only two said, "Oh shit, what now?"

That's when I said, "You are all off duty until 5 p.m. If I were you guys, I would hit the john, take a shower, get a nap and regain the strength you expended over the last twenty hours. Congratulations on a job well done!"

\* \* \*

On September 10, just before dusk, our battalion's adjutant called Sergeant Corson and told him that two of the battalion's men had been sightseeing, taking photos of the bombed bridge over the Danube in the town of Lovi-Sad, when they were shot at by young German kids. In the last days of the war, scraping the bottom of the barrel, Hitler had called on children to defend his crumbling regime. We called these kids, some as young as nine, "Hitler's werewolves," and it looked like a few were still in action.

The adjutant told me that Company D should be issued armed weapons whenever our men were expected to be late or just plain out after dark. The Seventh Army had already warned their divisions to take decisive actions against any armed children. They were to be treated like armed adults.

The war was over and everyone knew it. German parents did what they could to stop the werewolves. But during the last few weeks our battalion had spread out near the Danube River bridge, where werewolves tended to hang out in armed groups. This meant our troops were continually on alert with loaded weapons. The werewolves would prowl in the early evening, picking off careless officers and soldiers, knifing them, attacking and shooting them with machine pistols, booby-trapping paths with grenades. As Sergeant Joe would say, "You are just as dead if iced by a ten-year-old kid as you would be if shot by a forty-five-year-old combat-experienced kraut." Actually, I thought that being killed by a ten-year-old kid would make you feel even more dead and wasted.

Some of the werewolves were mighty handy with grenades and guns. You really haven't been scared until five or six kids surprise you by each throwing a potato-masher grenade across a narrow canal with a perfect arch, slowly sailing toward you, giving you a horrible feeling that your future will end in three seconds.

Our company's troops had experienced a few scary encounters with werewolves, one of which resulted in the death of a soldier about three weeks after we were ordered to start turning in all battle equipment—guns, grenades, etc—in preparation for our departure to the U.S.A. We were in a caravan of trucks, tracks, and jeeps traveling through many small towns. We passed Heidelberg University and a few bombed-out areas where the caravan was flagged down by MPs for inspections. At one of these stops, the driver of our lead jeep waved to three kids, a girl and two boys, who were standing nearby. One of the kids tossed a concussion grenade into the passenger's side of his jeep, killing him. To be killed weeks after the war was over—sad!

\* \* \*

We were all ready for the long-delayed party, dance, crap game and music that Sergeant Lou had promised for so long. It was to feature wine, German beer, and Lou Dinucci's homemade pretzels. Three of us were discussing the werewolf problem when, lo and behold, I received a call from battalion. It seems some men had been fired on by a group of werewolves near the bombed bridge at Novi-Sad. Could we clean up the problem?

I told Lou to stay in charge of his café while Sergeant Joe and I looked into the situation. I figured it was probably just a false alarm and would be a quick turnaround for us. Sergeant Joe drove our jeep. It sill had two loaded machine guns in it. It was growing dark as we left for the wrecked bridge, which was approximately three miles from our hotel. The roads had been strafed and bombed a few times, making it necessary to drive slowly, especially with only our small "cat-eye" lights as illumination. Cat-eye lights were standard on all army vehicles. The regular bulbs were covered by tar tape.

We parked near one of the bridge's superstructure supports, a large, very dark concrete area surrounded by bombed-out walls and piles of rubble. There was a very chilly breeze coming off the wide, strong current of the river. I told Joe that I would go north along the crumbled wall and that he should go south. We both loaded our machine guns and removed our locks, getting prepared for any surprise or emergency.

When we were about thirty or forty yards apart, both stumbling over debris and wreckage, I could hear and see a young couple hugging in a dark corner of a brick wall. I flashed my light toward Sergeant Smith and yelled for him to join me. Then I approached the couple, who turned out to be not werewolves but a young Czechoslovakian girl and a young American private from the "Hell on Wheels" battalion. I told them that no one was allowed in the area after dark.

I turned as Joe approached and started over to our jeep. We both had our guns hanging to our sides. I told Joe that they were both very young, that the soldier was from the "Hell on Wheels" battalion and drunk, and that he should be written up as a danger to other soldiers. Before either of us could react, the young soldier brought his hand from his back pocket, holding a cocked German Luger and shoved it into my gut, hard. Joe and I were both holding our machine guns, but the kid's gun was in control. He snarled in a very scary way that he was going to kill me, because I had just made his sweetheart go home too early.

That was BS, but this private, fresh from the States, was in charge. A terrible thought flashed through my mind. Here I had survived a war, and was about to be killed by some stupid jackass. The beam from Joe's flashlight hit my arm, showing my first sergeant's stripes, and the kid said, "I always wanted to kill a frigging first sergeant."

I looked at Joe to see what was next and he was right on time, "Kid, you don't even know what a first sergeant is. You are a G.D. snotnosed bag of s***! And a noncombatant." Inwardly I groaned. Joe was making the situation even worse. But then I heard Joe say, "Yes, sir." And I became aware of a second lieutenant standing behind the kid. Joe had intentionally spelled out our problem to the lieutenant

Then the lieutenant yelled, "Private, you small bucket of turds, give me that G.D. gun, butt first. You are a disgrace to the battalion."

At this point I could only think, *Hell, this guy has nothing to lose. The Luger is in my gut. If he aggravates the kid, I'll be the only loser. Even Joe couldn't lose, and what's more he still owes me $110 from our last crap game!* But the lieutenant snatched the Luger from the kid, stuck it in his belt, and ordered him to report to the charge of quarters at his headquarters.

Then looking at Sergeant Joe and me, the lieutenant said that it I wanted him to, he would put the private up on court martial charges. He told me to stop by his headquarters and ask for Second Lieutenant Andrews. Glancing first at Joe, I said, "Lieutenant, I don't ever want to see you or that son of a bitch again as long as I live! Good bye!"

As they started to walk back toward town, and we walked in the opposite direction to our jeep, Sergeant Joe used his flashlight on me and started to laugh, saying, "Durk, did you know that you wet your pants? Both pant legs are soaking wet."

I said, "Yes, you peckerhead. I was the first one to notice it about three-quarters of an hour ago."

"Oh, this was one for the books," Joe said. "A real knee-slapper if I ever heard one. Wait till I tell Dinucci and he tells Gargano, that old loudmouth!"

# 10

# GOING HOME

If I had asked my company clerk, Sergeant Charley Corson, once it seemed like I had asked him a hundred times to take one of our jeeps over to the railroad yard. "Go to the yard master's office and have him show you our string of boxcars. Pick out the cleanest, newest and best car for our trip to Camp Lucky Strike." Finally we were leaving for Marseilles, on the southern coast of France.

"Sergeant Corson," I said, "this boxcar is going to be our home for about one week of damned cold weather. Make sure there is a stove and no cracks or holes in the floor. But before you leave for the railroad yard, take your men and see if they can rummage in the officers' rooms and confiscate four or five duffel bags to fill with briquettes for our stove. Most important of all, I want those men to put my innerspring mattress in a corner of the car." That mattress had been removed from what was supposedly Marshal Goering's bed in his grand hunting lodge.

Here's where I kicked my butt mentally all the way to Camp Lucky Strike in Marseilles.

The first time I looked at our boxcar, it was in the middle of a very long string of similar railroad cars. It contained a very small homemade rusty stove with a broken lid and a bent, cracked stovepipe improperly fitted into the roof. You could see stars through the holes around the stack and it was very drafty. But on the side of the car there was a sign in French that said, "8 horses, 40 men." I liked that. Finally, we *were* the cavalry. We had finally caught up with the horses.

I spent most of the morning loading, checking, and rechecking the car, making sure it was clean and that there were no holes in the floor. One end of it was stacked totally to the ceiling with duffle bags that were jammed full of coal briquettes. If we didn't burn the damned boxcar down or choke to death from all the smoke, we'd be damned lucky.

One side of the boxcar held my mattress, already covered with ten or twelve duffel bags holding extra clothes, coats, guns, knives, flags, all types of wines, and items to barter whenever the train was forced to stop. The sliding door would not close tightly. The weather was bitter cold and because the windows in the sliding door had been blacked out, it was very gloomy, although we did have two large swinging lanterns. Most of the floor was covered by about twelve inches of fairly clean straw.

As we left, I was lucky to be pulled into the car as the engine began a very slow movement through the bombed-out rail yard, backing up, going around, stopping while another locomotive used our exit and went out on the line. Some of the stops were bone jarring. During one of them, we lost two idiot soldiers who were hanging out their sliding doors trying to entice a few pretty young girls to go on a dream trip to Marseilles.

At one point I jumped from our door and fast-walked up nearly to the engine to determine what was wrong. I was alerted to the problems of the railroad. We supposedly had sixteen exit rails. But five trains were coming in. Four other tracks still had bombed wrecks covering them that the engineers needed to bypass. The rest of the tracks had sections with no ties, half-filled bomb craters and potholes.

Even with those problems, I never understood why it took an engineer four hours to pull a string of boxcars out of a freight yard. But finally we were on our way to Marseilles—very slowly. As we left the yard, I began mentally to kick both Sergeant Corson and myself in the butt. I did that continually for the next six and a half days, in fact, every time I looked at our stove. It didn't emit heat, it only smoked. The draft from the holes around the stovepipe made it even colder. And the damned boxcar had two flat wheels. Every time they rotated at the curves, they would jar the hell out of your teeth.

It was one hell of a long distance from Munich to Marseilles in a "first-class railcoach." And when you ride in a boxcar that has transported horses, no matter how hard you try to clean it out, the odor is bound to linger. At least it lingered in our twelve inches of straw, which had definitely been previously used by some horses. But we kept moving, listening to the clackety clack, clackety clackety clack, clack, clack of the flat wheels. Then there was the bump, bumpity-bump and a soothing ka-bump every time the train stopped, which was about twenty or thirty times a day. Every time it did, GIs would pour out of every boxcar and try to trade their K rations to the villagers for wine, eggs, bread or anything a little village or countryside might have to trade. When we left Munich, every soldier had extra rations, wine, booze, shoes, clothes, blankets, and uniforms. When we reached Marseilles and fell out for roll call, the clothes on our back were the total extent of our wealth.

We did pick up speed, at one point alarmingly, after we reached France. I learned later that a couple of our sergeants had given the engineer and his assistant a little over a gallon and a half of good German grape wine, plus a couple of fifths of Three Feathers. Then, after escorting them into a half-empty coach where they were fed and kept drunk, the sergeants drove the train "full speed ahead—let's go home."

\* \* \*

Camp Lucky Strike in Marseilles had been erected near the top of one hell of a freezing, windy mountainside. It consisted of row upon row of holey, ripped, filthy, dirty, stinking, poorly erected pyramidal tents. When we got there, a forty- or fifty-mile-an-hour wind was blowing down those rows of tents twenty-four hours a day, with the weird sound of a million or so banshees. And the latrines! They were simply standing pieces of terra cotta pipes. The contact of our butts on the chipped concrete left much to be desired and the odor of the latrines seemed to cling to your body. Given the freezing wind and the fact that the latrines were on the opposite end of the road from our tent, we all had the urge to utilize the street instead. Every tent had one little stove, and was given just one little bucket of coal a day. It was too cold for sleep.

Finally, thank the Lord, we received word from our favorite rumormonger, Camp Lucky Strike's PA system, that the ship we would take home was only twelve hours out of port. The *Zanesville Victory* would dock during the night. After that, its captain's decision to weigh anchor would be dependent on our degree of readiness. But, realizing our departure was now a certainty, most of our men had taken a vote to spend one more night in France, especially Marseilles.

Before we left Lucky Strike, I received master medic's kits, the type that medics hand out to every serviceman when they go on the prowl. After passing out a kit to each man, I warned them that every man would be given the old "raincoat inspection" by the ship's doctor and medics before the ship left port. Any man with venereal disease would not ship out, and would serve one extra year with our occupation forces.

By 1 a.m. most of my men were scattered down in the tough bars of Marseilles. We had not always been completely accepted in the French towns we had been though, but tonight we were fed their best food and booze. We were the "hero soldiers" who had given them back their homes, country and dignity. We heard the word "merci" over and over again, often with tears.

Sergeant Jimmy Adams had been born and raised in the mountains of Tennessee and poor Jimmy sure missed his mountains. He was six feet six inches tall and he tried to speak what he called "Tennessee-French" in downtown Marseilles. At one point, we were all in one of the largest cutthroat bars in a tough part of town. Jim was drinking straight vodka. Next to him, Sergeant Corson was on wine. Neither had the slightest idea where they were.

The bar was one big party and on the other side of Jim there was a very happy Frenchman who could not speak a bit of English. When he saw a wedding party pass by the bar, Jim asked the Frenchman, "Who was that?"

The Frenchman said, "Je ne sais pas."

Jim nodded and started drinking from Corson's jar of wine. A minute or two later, a funeral procession came by, and poor soused Sergeant Adams said to the very drunk Frenchman, "Wass dat?"

The Frenchman said, "Je ne sais pas."

Jim mumbled, "Poor guy. Sure as hell didn't last long, did he? Huh?" Burp. "Aum schick." And Adams was very, very "schick."

Finally we shook hands all around, staggered back towards Lucky Strike and the job of throwing out our trash and getting ready to depart. It was our turn, finally. Our battalion was scheduled to be the next contingent to board ship.

\* \* \*

After breakfast the next cold December morning, I had our total company assembled, most of them coherent and all of them aware of our imminent departure for the States. They were a bunch of very happy soldiers. I alerted every man to be correctly packed and mentally alert for our call to board. The moves would be A Company, B Company, C Company and finally our Company D, with battalion headquarters leading the way and designating the best staterooms as theirs. About a week before this, our officers had been transferred to the Air Corps and flown home. Their replacement officers were all rear-echelon desk warriors, to Sergeant Smith "numb nuts" and to Felix "plain ball-busters."

As we got prepared to board the ship, the captain announced that we were now subject to the Navy's "gang-plank rule"—"Once aboard, you stay aboard. No excuses!"

Last night did not exist. After we finally boarded, I spent the balance of the day inspecting duffel bags and checking out the men's readiness for our departure. Everyone had passed the somewhat casual medical exam before boarding, but as we were about to sail one of the men admitted to a case of scabies. Extremely contagious, this usually called for total isolation. Without turning him in, we did our best, but by the time we reached New York probably sixty percent of the crew and soldiers had caught it.

Troop ships were never designed for comfort. Even on the *Queen Mary* cots were stacked ten high, with just enough room between them to allow you to breathe. But on the *ZV*, believe it or not, not only our lieutenant but also First Sergeant Durkin and his noncoms were posted to staterooms.

The next morning we were all in high spirits. One of Gargano's men laughingly asked him if he was still going to have trouble with seasickness, remembering how the sergeant had spent nearly the whole trip coming over on the *Queen Mary* throwing up. We all remembered—if you were standing near him, you too became seasick. I joked that I had asked Sergeant Smith to beg that Gargano be sent back by plane or glider, but it hadn't worked out.

Gargano swore over and over again that he would not be seasick on the way home. By this time he had been dealing cards for about an hour when the ship's captain announced over the PA system, "Now hear this, cast off aft,"

Everyone started to cheer, Sergeant Gargano the loudest, screaming, "I'm not seasick!"

Then the captain said, "Now hear this, cast off forward." The ship's engines started to throb and Gargano heaved!

Marseilles, goodbye! Everyone was up at the rails waving noisily. As the city grew faint on the horizon, we stood around waiting for Sergeant Dinucci and a hungover Sergeant Adams to get us some breakfast. What we got was mainly coffee and more coffee. Every duffel bag on the ship, at least those from our company, concealed two or three full gallon jugs of homemade booze. Most of us had a couple of bottles of Three Feathers stuffed into the arms of our Army overcoats. Sergeant Dinucci and his cooks, I mean crooks, had smuggled them aboard and then hidden them in the lifeboats. We posted guards, planning to protect our lifeboats from the real guards on the *ZV* crew.

The weather was beautiful when we set sail. But by late morning of our second day on board it changed and became cold and windy.

The *ZV* was rolling up and down and from one side to the other. The ship's captain alerted us on the PA system that we were to utilize the "man-overboard" handgrips on the railing, gripping them tightly as we moved around the outside of the ship.

The men grew tired of playing cards, and we were all soon exhausted by the stormy weather. The *Zanesville Victory* went through some blinding snowstorms; Sergeant Gargano was not the only one who was seasick. We were all boat sick. I remember in the middle of one storm, Sergeant Joe Rich started singing a ballad that Woody Guthrie wrote, whose refrain went, "Tell me, what were their names." Most of us were yelling back at Joe, "What in the hell *were* their names?" And we tried to remember the names of people like the lieutenant whom Lieutenant Purdie had replaced. But in the words of Felix, if he wasn't a civilian, he was a pain in the ass.

The ship skirted Barcelona, Valencia and Malaga, Spain, passing Gibraltar at night through the straight into the Atlantic.

As we entered the Atlantic Ocean I requested a standing-room-only meeting in the ship's library. We talked about where we had been, what we had done, and agreed to a man that we would never forget the men left behind. Sergeant Gargano recommended that we meet at 2 p.m. each day for a bull session, to share each other's memories and future plans. All were welcome.

Sergeant Gargano was first with a realistic memory for all—D-Day. We remembered crossing the channel on that LCVP, and waiting thirty-six hours to off-load while high-flying German bombers, too high for us to reach, dropped bombs blindly, hoping for a lucky hit on one of the LCs. We remembered how dark and cold it was, and how scared we all were. We remembered hoping that we wouldn't fall into the water among all the floating bodies from the invasion.

We laughed as we remembered Lieutenant Purdie and Sergeant Joe Smith's plaid suit and high hat and how he looked like a "California clap doctor." And we remembered that he had promised to wear the suit and the hat to our first reunion in New York.

We remembered the men we left behind.

\* \* \*

Our eighth day on the *ZV* was another stormy, rolling day. The captain announced that we were just two days from "port of call." A few of us were gathered in the ship's library having coffee. We had just been told that Lieutenant Viola, who had remained in Marseilles, had been promoted to captain. We were all pleased, because he was just about everyone's favorite officer. Sergeant Gargano exploded with laughter and said, "Do you remember when Lieutenant Viola made that early morning comfort stop and was squatting bare ass over the straddle trench, humming to himself, when the two lovely young mam-selles swinging their pails as they came up the path suddenly spotted the lieutenant and cheerfully greeted him with, 'Bon jour, monsieur Lieutenant,' and giggling wished him a good day as the red-faced lieutenant pulled up his drawers and stepped in the trench, where he remained until they were out of sight?"

Gargano and Felix recalled going to the lieutenant's assistance and laughing so hard they nearly ended up in the trench with him. Bad things *do* happen to good people.

"Sergeant Gargano," I shook my head and growled, "the Good Lord must have an entire choir of angels assigned just to keep your dumb asses out of trouble!"

\* \* \*

We got into a real argument about how much money the U.S. had spent on the war. Someone had read that lend-lease aid alone had amounted to $48,601,365,000. The numbers staggered us, and some of us were damned mad. With that kind of money being shipped overseas, we all wanted a raise. The argument was never settled on board, although we did quiet down when someone said something none of us could believe. He swore up and down that he had heard that we could all go to college free if we wanted to!

\* \* \*

During World War II, the homelands of more than three-quarters of the population of the earth had felt the crush of the heel of Mars. More than a hundred million people—one out of every twenty human beings on the globe—had been engaged in the fighting forces of belligerent nations. The final records of World War II as set forth in the participants' tally sheets, challenge the imagination. The official lists of numbers killed and wounded are a tragic commentary on civilization: more than 20 million casualties, and 30 million more men, women and children driven from homes left in ruins.

The cost of this war for survival, with its destruction, devastation and economic losses, has been estimated at the sum of $1 trillion. The wealth of the world, with all of its resources, industrial power, and manpower, had been concentrated on destruction. Nations had accumulated debt that far exceeded all of the money in the world when the war began The responsibility for meeting this obligation was placed upon future generations.

This was the price we paid for human freedom. The amount of money consumed in this war was sufficient to build a home for every family in the world, or to give an education to every child on earth. It was far greater than all the money ever expended for schools, churches, and hospitals since the beginning of the human race.

Billions of words have been written about World War II. Now I have added a few more, about the war as seen through the eyes of a twenty-two-year-old combat first sergeant of cavalry. It is true that the winning side always writes the history, but I'm damned glad I was on the winning side!

\* \* \*

We had the run of the ship's library while we were on board, and many of us used it to read about what we had participated in during the past three years. I remember reading a passage from an undelivered speech President Roosevelt had written shortly before his death:

*"Today we are faced with the pre-eminent fact that, if civilization is to survive, we must cultivate the science of human relationships— the ability of all peoples, of all kinds, to live together and work together in the same world at peace..."*

\* \* \*

After we were off-loaded at our port of entry on December 24, we were bussed to nearby Fort Monmouth. When we went to eat, we were told, "Just ask for it, no matter what. Anything you have wanted for the last year or so." I wanted a big lemon meringue pie and a fresh cold quart of cow's milk. I still remember how good they tasted—all I had dreamed of and more.

I shared that meal with a lieutenant who ate like a hungry horse and then announced that no soldier would be allowed off of our base until after being discharged. It was still light when I whistled my men out for formation. I relayed the lieutenant's order that no one could leave our base until severance on December 27. This was greeted by a mutinous uproar. Then I pointed out to them that most of us had been away from home for a couple of years. And from where we were standing, they had to walk about one and a half miles to get to busses, taxis and highways. "Personally," I said, "I'm going home tonight, come hell or high water. You do what you want to do. But you will fall in with formation on December 27 for your release from the Army or you will be AWOL and the MPs will escort you to Leavenworth. Any questions? If not, I wish you all a Merry Christmas. Now get out of here. I'll see you December twenty-seventh."

I took off like a bat out of hell with everyone else in a mad exodus for home. In minutes I was on a bus heading to dear old South Jersey— at last!

*I'll Be Home for Christmas.*

# EPILOGUE

Since I began this book, the size of Company D has diminished considerably. Each reunion finds fewer vets in attendance. At our last reunion in the fall of '99, there were eleven of us.

I was lucky. God blessed me with a fantastic company of men. Even Felix, it seems, became bored with civilian life and one afternoon at the local American Legion was talked into joining the Army Reserves. He ended up being activated and sent to Korea, where he was wounded and made permanent private first class. He also, as promised, made the front page of the local paper.

Having moved to Connecticut, I lost track of Felix. But on the rare occasions we met he always greeted me the same way. "Durkin, you rotten, no-good SOB, I've told everybody about you!"

Isn't it funny how some guys carry a grudge? In a lifetime, if we are lucky, we meet someone who truly marches to his own drummer. He may be exasperating, constipating, and may even drive you over the edge. Though you sure as hell don't want him to know it, you can't help but love him.

Among those who have passed on are Staff Sergeant Joe Smith and Permanent PFC Felix Spizzica. I'm sure by now, with Joe egging him on, Felix has made a deal with Saint Peter. "When Sergeant Durkin comes knockin', don't let that SOB in!"

I repeat, "Some guys carry a grudge!"

Printed in the United States
49178LVS00002B/232-372

9 781413 753745